THE MAGIC OF HOLIDAY BAKING

Sweet Recipes for a Joyful Season

HANNAH REED

Table of Contents

3

Chapter 1: Welcome to the Christmas Baking Season

There is something magical about the Christmas season that brings us together in the kitchen, creating treats infused with warmth and tradition. Baking for the holidays is more than just a culinary task; it's a time-honored ritual that weaves together family, friends, and neighbors in the joy of preparing and sharing festive treats. The act of baking is, in essence, a celebration—one where we mix, whisk, and knead not just ingredients, but also love and gratitude into every batch of cookies and every slice of cake.

During the holidays, baking connects generations. Recipes passed down from our grandparents or inspired by old family traditions remind us of childhood memories and simpler times. Whether it's the smell of fresh gingerbread, the shimmer of powdered sugar on snowball cookies, or the first taste of a rich fruitcake, Christmas baking captures the spirit of giving and community. As we share these homemade treasures with others, we create new memories that extend the warmth of Christmas beyond the kitchen, reminding us that baking is truly a gift of the heart.

Essential Ingredients for Festive Baking

Christmas baking is all about creating rich, comforting flavors that bring holiday cheer into every bite. Stocking up on high-quality ingredients is the first step to making unforgettable treats. Here are a few ingredients that play starring roles in holiday recipes, lending distinct flavors and textures to classic Christmas creations.

6

- **Spices**: Warm spices such as cinnamon, nutmeg, cloves, ginger, and allspice are essentials in Christmas baking. They're often found in holiday staples like gingerbread, fruitcake, and spice cookies, adding depth and a cozy aroma.
- **Nuts**: Almonds, pecans, walnuts, and hazelnuts are popular choices, adding crunch and richness. They're perfect in cookies, pastries, and brittle, or as decorative toppings.
- **Dried Fruits**: Raisins, cranberries, cherries, and dates bring sweetness and texture to festive baked goods. Dried fruit is often soaked in brandy or rum for traditional cakes and puddings, adding complexity to their flavor.
- **Chocolate**: From dark chocolate to white chocolate, chocolate is a holiday favorite for adding richness and indulgence. It's a key ingredient in everything from fudge to cookies and cakes.
- **Sweeteners**: Sugar is a staple, but you'll also want to have brown sugar and powdered sugar for holiday baking. Brown sugar adds a caramel-like richness, and powdered sugar is perfect for icings and snowy finishes on cookies.
- **Butters and Creams**: Butter is the cornerstone of most holiday baking, lending richness and tenderness to pastries, cookies, and cakes. Heavy cream, sour cream, and even cream cheese are also commonly used to create soft, moist textures.

Stocking the Pantry: Must-Have Items for the Holidays

Creating a well-stocked holiday pantry ensures you'll have everything on hand for spur-of-the-moment baking. Here's a checklist of essentials that will make your holiday baking go smoothly.

Baking Staples

- **Flours**: All-purpose flour is a baking staple, but consider adding cake flour and bread flour for more specialized recipes.
- **Sugars**: White granulated sugar, brown sugar, and powdered sugar are essential for various recipes. Keep molasses and honey on hand as well.
- **Leavening Agents**: Baking powder, baking soda, and yeast are necessary to make your treats rise and stay light and fluffy.

Holiday Additions

- **Extracts and Flavors**: Vanilla extract is a must-have, and almond, peppermint, and rum extracts add festive notes.
- **Spices**: Cinnamon, nutmeg, cloves, ginger, and allspice should be fresh and high-quality, as they're used extensively in holiday recipes.
- **Nuts and Dried Fruits**: Stock up on nuts (pecans, walnuts, almonds) and dried fruits (cranberries, raisins, cherries, apricots).
- **Chocolate and Cocoa**: Keep a mix of baking chocolate, white chocolate, cocoa powder, and chocolate chips for various recipes.
- **Dairy**: Butter, heavy cream, and cream cheese are holiday essentials, along with whole milk and eggs.

Having these basics ready means you can dive into the holiday spirit whenever inspiration strikes, without running to the store for last-minute items.

Key Tools and Equipment for Holiday Baking Success

Equipping your kitchen with the right tools can transform holiday baking from a chore into a delightful experience. Here's a guide to some essential equipment that will make your Christmas baking smooth, efficient, and enjoyable.

Basic Equipment

- **Mixers**: A stand mixer is invaluable for making doughs, batters, and frostings, while a hand mixer is useful for smaller tasks.
- **Measuring Cups and Spoons**: Precise measurements are key to baking success, so keep both dry and liquid measuring cups on hand.
- **Mixing Bowls**: A set of different-sized mixing bowls is essential, especially when preparing large batches or multiple recipes.

Specialty Tools

- **Rolling Pin and Cookie Cutters**: A sturdy rolling pin is a must for pie crusts and rolled cookies, and holiday-shaped cookie cutters add a festive touch.
- **Piping Bags and Tips**: For decorating cookies and cakes, a variety of piping tips allow for detailed, beautiful designs.
- **Silicone Baking Mats and Parchment Paper**: Both are great for non-stick baking and make cleanup easier, especially for cookies and delicate pastries.

9

Baking Pans

- **Baking Sheets**: Quality baking sheets are perfect for cookies, while rimmed sheets work well for bars and sheet cakes.
- **Cake Pans and Pie Dishes**: Have an assortment of round cake pans, square pans, and pie dishes ready for cakes, cheesecakes, and pies.
- **Loaf Pans and Muffin Tins**: Loaf pans are great for bread and pound cakes, while muffin tins are perfect for cupcakes, muffins, and mini treats.

Using high-quality, reliable equipment will ensure your baked goods turn out beautifully, making your baking experience both satisfying and stress-free.

Understanding Festive Flavors and Aromas

Christmas baking is a sensory experience, with flavors and aromas that evoke warmth, nostalgia, and joy. Certain ingredients have become synonymous with the holiday season, not only for their taste but for the emotions they inspire.

Classic Christmas Flavors

- **Spiced and Warm Flavors**: Cinnamon, nutmeg, cloves, and ginger add warmth and depth. Their cozy, aromatic qualities make them holiday favorites.
- **Citrus**: Orange and lemon zest brighten up rich treats, bringing a hint of freshness and balance.
- **Vanilla and Almond**: Vanilla is a comforting, familiar flavor, and almond extract adds a distinct, festive note, especially in European-inspired holiday cookies.

- **Peppermint**: A holiday staple, peppermint adds a fresh, cool flavor that pairs well with chocolate. It's perfect in cookies, hot cocoa, and ice cream.

Aromas That Define the Season

- **Fresh-Baked Gingerbread**: Few aromas are as closely associated with Christmas as the spicy-sweet smell of gingerbread baking in the oven.
- **Roasting Nuts**: Toasted nuts give off a rich, earthy aroma that complements baked goods and candy, adding a touch of decadence.
- **Simmering Caramel**: The deep, sugary scent of caramel evokes the feeling of indulgence, found in everything from toffee to caramel sauces.

By combining these flavors and aromas, holiday baking becomes a sensory journey that fills the kitchen—and the home—with an ambiance of Christmas magic. Each treat prepared is a celebration of these timeless flavors, a taste of nostalgia, and an invitation to gather, share, and savor every moment.

In this chapter, we've embraced the essence of holiday baking: the joy of creating, the pleasure of sharing, and the delightful anticipation that comes with every bite. As we venture into this season of warmth and wonder, let's carry forward the traditions, make new memories, and savor the spirit of Christmas, one delicious treat at a time.

Chapter 2: Preparations for a Smooth Holiday Baking Experience

The Christmas baking season can be one of the most joyful—and busiest—times in the kitchen. From family favorites to intricate new recipes, holiday baking can quickly become overwhelming without the right preparation. This chapter covers foundational baking techniques, professional decorating tips, and clever hacks to keep things fun and stress-free.

Mastering Basic Baking Techniques

Even the simplest holiday treats can be transformed into something spectacular with solid foundational skills. By mastering basic baking techniques, you can create consistently delicious and beautiful baked goods every time.

1. Measuring Ingredients Accurately

- **Weighing vs. Measuring by Volume**: For precise baking, weighing ingredients, especially flour, is ideal. If using measuring cups, be careful not to over-pack ingredients. Fluff flour before scooping, and level it with a knife to avoid dense results.
- **Wet and Dry Ingredients**: Use liquid measuring cups for wet ingredients and dry measuring cups for dry ingredients. This small detail can make a big difference in the accuracy of your recipes.

2. Mixing Techniques

- **Creaming Butter and Sugar**: Properly creaming butter and sugar adds air to the batter, creating a light texture in cookies and cakes. Beat until the mixture is light and fluffy, usually for about 3-5 minutes.
- **Folding**: Folding is essential for light, airy textures, especially with egg whites or whipped cream. Gently fold ingredients together with a spatula, using sweeping motions to prevent deflating the mixture.
- **Kneading Dough**: Kneading develops gluten, which gives structure to breads and some pastries. To knead by hand, fold the dough onto itself, then push it away with the heel of your hand, repeating until smooth and elastic.

3. Temperature Control

- **Room Temperature Ingredients**: Many recipes call for room-temperature butter, eggs, and milk to ensure smooth mixing and even baking. Let ingredients sit out for about 30 minutes before starting.
- **Preheating the Oven**: Always preheat your oven to ensure even baking from the start. Use an oven thermometer if possible, as many ovens run hot or cold.
- **Cooling Baked Goods Properly**: Let baked goods cool in their pans for the specified time before transferring them to a wire rack. Cooling properly prevents them from becoming soggy or breaking.

4. Testing for Doneness

- **Cookies**: Most cookies are done when the edges are lightly browned and the center looks set. They will continue to firm up as they cool.
- **Cakes**: Insert a toothpick in the center. If it comes out clean or with a few crumbs, the cake is ready. If it comes out with batter, bake a few minutes longer.
- **Bread**: Tap the bottom of the loaf; a hollow sound usually means it's fully baked.

Mastering these techniques provides a strong foundation, helping you create treats that are consistent in flavor and texture, so you can move on to decorating and styling with confidence.

Tips for Decorating Like a Pro

The visual appeal of holiday treats is just as important as their taste. Decorating like a pro can seem daunting, but with the right techniques and tools, anyone can create beautiful cookies, cakes, and pastries that look as good as they taste.

1. Understanding Basic Icing Techniques

- **Royal Icing**: Perfect for cookies, royal icing is made from powdered sugar, egg whites, and a bit of water or lemon juice. It dries hard, making it ideal for detailed designs. Thin it out for "flooding" (covering the cookie with a smooth layer) and use thicker icing for piping details.
- **Buttercream Frosting**: A classic for cakes and cupcakes, buttercream can be easily colored and piped into beautiful designs. Use a variety of piping tips to create different patterns, from roses to ruffles.

- **Glaze Icing**: Made from powdered sugar and milk, glaze icing is simpler and ideal for drizzling over scones, pastries, or bundt cakes.

2. Using Piping Bags and Tips

- **Selecting the Right Tips**: Star tips are great for rosettes and swirls, round tips for polka dots and lines, and leaf tips for creating foliage designs. Experiment with a few tip shapes to find the best designs for your treats.
- **Practice Piping**: Piping can take practice. Before decorating your cookies or cakes, practice on parchment paper to get comfortable with the pressure and motion required for each design.
- **Reusable or Disposable Piping Bags**: Disposable bags are convenient for multi-colored icings, while reusable bags are great for larger projects.

3. Adding Decorative Touches

- **Sprinkles and Edible Glitter**: A sprinkle of holiday-colored nonpareils or edible glitter adds festive flair. Go for metallic accents, reds, greens, or even snowflake-shaped sprinkles for an extra touch.
- **Dragees and Candies**: These tiny metallic balls and candies can add a luxurious, textured effect to cakes and cookies.
- **Piping Patterns**: For intricate designs, try drawing patterns with an edible marker as a guide. Then, trace over your outline with icing.

4. Creating a Festive Presentation

- **Using Seasonal Colors**: Red, green, gold, and silver are classic Christmas colors. Think about how these colors will contrast and complement each other on your finished treats.
- **Holiday-Themed Shapes**: Holiday-themed cookie cutters (stars, Christmas trees, snowflakes) make cookies look festive even with minimal decoration.

Professional-looking decorations can be simple and elegant or detailed and intricate. Practice and a few essential tools can elevate any treat to a festive masterpiece.

Essential Baking Hacks for the Holidays

With the busy nature of holiday baking, a few clever hacks can save time and simplify the process. From ingredient swaps to time-saving tricks, these holiday baking hacks are all about maximizing efficiency without sacrificing quality.

1. Quick Ingredient Softening

- **Butter**: To quickly soften butter, cut it into small cubes and let it sit for 10–15 minutes at room temperature. Alternatively, place it between two sheets of wax paper and roll it out with a rolling pin to soften faster.
- **Eggs**: If you forgot to bring eggs to room temperature, place them in a bowl of warm (not hot) water for 5–10 minutes.

2. Preventing Cookie Spread

- **Chilling the Dough**: To prevent cookies from spreading, chill the dough for at least 30 minutes before baking. Cold dough holds its shape better and produces thicker, chewier cookies.

- **Use Parchment Paper**: Line baking sheets with parchment paper to prevent sticking, even baking, and easier cleanup.

3. Easy Pie Crust Perfection

- **Keep Ingredients Cold**: Cold butter and cold water are essential for a flaky pie crust. Consider chilling your mixing bowl and even your rolling pin for best results.
- **Roll Between Wax Paper**: Rolling pie dough between two sheets of wax paper prevents sticking and makes transferring the crust to the pie dish easier.

4. Faster Cleanup and Organization

- **Silicone Mats for Easy Cleanup**: Silicone baking mats reduce sticking and make cleanup easier, especially for messy items like caramel.
- **Organize Ingredients Before Starting**: Measure out ingredients before beginning, often called "mise en place," to avoid last-minute scrambles.
- **Use Binder Clips for Precision**: Use binder clips on parchment paper to keep it from sliding on the baking sheet, making it easier to pipe or decorate precisely.

5. Repurposing Leftover Ingredients

- **Egg Whites and Yolks**: Use extra egg whites for meringues, or egg yolks for rich custards or ice creams.

- **Leftover Dough Scraps**: Roll scraps of pie or pastry dough with cinnamon and sugar for quick cinnamon twists—perfect for a snack or breakfast treat.

6. DIY Festive Packaging

- **Make Your Own Cookie Gift Boxes**: Use muffin liners in a small box to hold individual cookies or treats. Line with parchment or wax paper and finish with a festive ribbon for a beautiful presentation.
- **Personalize with Labels and Tags**: Label jars or bags with handwritten or printed tags, adding a touch of personalization to holiday treats that make them memorable gifts.

With these hacks and tips in your holiday toolkit, you're ready to bake with ease, efficiency, and creativity. Embrace the preparation process, let the holiday spirit guide you, and remember that sometimes the smallest tricks can make the biggest difference in making your holiday baking stress-free and enjoyable.

Troubleshooting Common Baking Issues

Baking is both an art and a science, and minor changes in ingredients, temperature, or technique can result in issues with texture, flavor, or appearance. Knowing how to troubleshoot these common baking problems will help you stay calm under pressure and ensure that your treats turn out perfectly every time.

1. Cookies Spreading Too Much

- **Possible Cause**: Dough that's too warm or too high in butter content can cause cookies to spread excessively.
- **Solution**: Chill cookie dough for at least 30 minutes before baking. Using parchment paper or silicone baking mats also helps reduce spreading. Measure flour accurately, as too little flour can cause the dough to spread too thin.

2. Cakes Sinking in the Middle

- **Possible Cause**: Overmixing, underbaking, or too much leavening (baking powder/soda) can lead to sinking.
- **Solution**: Mix batter just until ingredients are combined to avoid overworking the gluten. Ensure the oven is preheated to the correct temperature, and avoid opening the door too early, as the drop in temperature can cause cakes to collapse. Use fresh leavening agents for best results, as expired ones lose their potency.

3. Dry or Crumbly Texture in Cakes and Muffins

- **Possible Cause**: Overbaking, too much flour, or too little fat or liquid can cause baked goods to become dry.
- **Solution**: Set a timer and check baked goods a few minutes before the suggested time. Use a toothpick to test doneness; if it comes out with a few crumbs, it's done. Accurately measure flour and avoid scooping directly from the bag, as this can lead to excess flour. Incorporate ingredients like sour cream, yogurt, or milk for added moisture.

4. Sticky or Dense Bread Dough

- **Possible Cause**: Sticky bread dough can be caused by using too much liquid, not enough kneading, or too little flour.
- **Solution**: Add small amounts of flour while kneading until the dough is workable but still slightly tacky. Knead thoroughly to develop gluten, which gives bread its structure. If the dough is too dense, check your yeast's expiration date, as old yeast may not rise properly.

5. Cracked or Lumpy Frosting

- **Possible Cause**: Butter that's too cold or adding liquid too quickly can cause frosting to crack or become lumpy.
- **Solution**: Start with room-temperature butter and add any milk or liquid a little at a time. Beat the frosting at medium speed until smooth and creamy. If lumps persist, strain the frosting or whip it longer to break up clumps.

6. Burnt Edges and Undercooked Centers

- **Possible Cause**: Uneven oven heat, incorrect baking pan sizes, or incorrect rack position can cause burnt edges.
- **Solution**: Position pans in the center of the oven and rotate halfway through baking if needed. Choose the correct pan size, as thinner batters in large pans cook unevenly. An oven thermometer can help ensure an accurate baking temperature, especially in older ovens.

7. Sticky or Tough Pie Crust

- **Possible Cause**: Overworking the dough, too much water, or using warm ingredients can cause pie crusts to be tough or sticky.

- **Solution**: Use cold butter and ice water to keep the dough cool, and avoid overmixing. Refrigerate the dough before rolling it out, and roll between two sheets of wax paper to prevent sticking. Handle the dough as little as possible to ensure a tender crust.

Being aware of these common issues and their solutions can help you navigate unexpected challenges, ensuring that your holiday baking goes smoothly and produces beautiful, delicious results.

Planning and Organizing Your Baking Schedule

The holiday baking season is often filled with an ambitious list of treats to bake, decorate, and share. Without a clear plan, it's easy to become overwhelmed by the volume of work. A well-organized baking schedule will allow you to manage time effectively, stay stress-free, and enjoy the process.

1. Make a Master List of All Recipes

- **Identify Must-Have Treats**: Begin by listing the absolute essentials—family favorites, treats for holiday parties, and giftable items. Consider choosing recipes that offer a variety of flavors, textures, and styles to keep things interesting.
- **Break Down Recipe Types**: Separate recipes into categories such as cookies, cakes, breads, pies, and candies. This will help you prioritize ingredients, baking times, and storage needs.

2. Organize Ingredients and Shopping

- **Create a Detailed Shopping List**: Once you have a master recipe list, make a shopping list of all required ingredients, organized by category (flour, sugar, spices, dairy). Double-check your pantry for items you may already have.

- **Buy in Bulk**: Purchasing items like flour, sugar, chocolate, and nuts in bulk can be more economical and ensures you won't run out halfway through baking.
- **Plan for Special Ingredients**: Certain holiday-specific ingredients (like candied fruits or edible glitter) may sell out quickly. Purchase these early in the season to avoid last-minute substitutions.

3. Plan for Make-Ahead Items

- **Freeze Doughs and Batters**: Many cookie doughs, like sugar or chocolate chip, can be prepared in advance and frozen. Simply shape the dough into logs or scoop portions, then freeze. When you're ready to bake, just thaw slightly and pop them in the oven.
- **Prepare Frosting and Fillings**: Buttercream frosting, ganache, and pie fillings can also be made ahead and stored in the refrigerator. This will save time and allow you to focus on assembling and decorating.
- **Bake in Stages**: Items like fruitcake or gingerbread, which improve with a bit of resting time, can be made a week or two in advance. Simply store in an airtight container until needed.

4. Schedule Baking Days and Rest Days

- **Set Aside Dedicated Baking Days**: Choose specific days for each baking category, such as one day for cookies, another for pies, and a third for breads. Block out enough time for preparation, baking, cooling, and cleanup.

- **Plan Rest Days**: Baking several days in a row can be tiring, so schedule rest days between large baking sessions. Use these days to clean up, reorganize your supplies, and prepare for the next round.
- **Organize by Bake Time and Complexity**: Begin with recipes that have longer bake times or require cooling before the next step. Quick-bake items like cookies or muffins can be scheduled last to make efficient use of the oven.

5. Coordinate with Freezer and Storage Space

- **Allocate Freezer Space**: Dedicate a section of your freezer for holiday baking items, particularly if you're making doughs, pies, or breads in advance. Label and date each item so it's easy to locate later.
- **Choose Proper Storage Containers**: Invest in airtight containers, tins, and holiday-themed packaging that keeps items fresh while adding a festive touch. Many cookies, cakes, and breads stay fresh longer when stored correctly.
- **Rotate Baked Goods**: For larger batches, try freezing a portion of baked goods to maintain freshness and prevent overcrowding on serving days. Freezing also makes it easy to pull out treats as needed for last-minute gatherings or gift-giving.

6. Plan for Decorating and Packaging

- **Set a Decorating Day**: If decorating cookies or cakes, set aside a day just for this task. Having all your baked items cooled and ready to go will make decorating less hectic.
- **Create a Gift Assembly Line**: If you're gifting treats, set up a workspace with all necessary packaging materials (boxes, tins, ribbons, tags). Batch items by type, so you can assemble and label each gift quickly and efficiently.

- **Involve Family or Friends**: Holiday baking can be a fun group activity. Enlist family or friends to help with decorating or packaging. Not only will this save time, but it also adds to the holiday spirit.

7. Use a Holiday Baking Calendar

- **Map Out Key Dates**: Use a calendar to mark when certain treats need to be baked, decorated, and gifted. Count backward from any major gatherings or gift exchanges to ensure items are at peak freshness when served.
- **Adjust as Needed**: The calendar is a guide, so be flexible if unexpected events arise. Keeping a list of backup recipes for quick treats (like brownies or bars) can be helpful if plans change or time becomes limited.

A well-thought-out baking schedule and troubleshooting know-how allow you to tackle holiday baking with confidence. By planning ahead, you'll avoid the last-minute rush and have plenty of time to savor the joy of creating and sharing holiday treats with those you love.

With these preparations, your holiday baking season will run smoothly and efficiently, leaving you with time to relax, enjoy the festivities, and share the fruits of your labor with family and friends.

Chapter 3: Recipes for Christmas Cakes

Christmas cakes are at the heart of holiday baking. These festive cakes bring warmth, nostalgia, and a touch of elegance to every holiday gathering. From the rich and boozy classic fruitcake to the aromatic gingerbread cake and the creamy, spiced eggnog bundt, these cakes embody the spirit of Christmas in every bite. Let's explore each of these recipes in detail.

Classic Christmas Fruitcake

The classic Christmas fruitcake is a staple of the holiday season, loved for its rich flavors and chewy textures. Made with dried fruits, nuts, spices, and often soaked in rum or brandy, this cake is best when made ahead of time to allow the flavors to meld together.

Ingredients:

- **Dried Fruits and Nuts**:
  - 1 cup raisins
  - 1 cup currants
  - 1/2 cup dried cherries
  - 1/2 cup dried apricots, chopped
  - 1/2 cup chopped dates
  - 1/4 cup crystallized ginger, chopped
  - 1/2 cup chopped pecans
  - 1/2 cup chopped walnuts
- **Liquor and Flavoring**:
  - 1/2 cup dark rum or brandy (for soaking fruit)
  - 1/2 cup orange juice
  - Zest of 1 orange
  - Zest of 1 lemon
- **Cake Batter**:
  - 1 cup unsalted butter, room temperature
  - 1 cup brown sugar
  - 4 large eggs, room temperature
  - 1 3/4 cups all-purpose flour
  - 1 tsp baking powder
  - 1/2 tsp salt
  - 1 tsp ground cinnamon
  - 1/2 tsp ground nutmeg
  - 1/2 tsp ground cloves
- **Finishing Touches**:
  - Additional rum or brandy for brushing

Instructions:

1. **Soak the Fruits**:
   - In a large bowl, combine raisins, currants, cherries, apricots, dates, and ginger with the rum and orange juice. Stir in the citrus zest. Cover and let soak for at least 8 hours or overnight for best results.
2. **Prepare the Cake Batter**:
   - Preheat your oven to 325°F (160°C). Grease a 9-inch cake pan and line it with parchment paper.
   - In a separate bowl, sift together the flour, baking powder, salt, cinnamon, nutmeg, and cloves.
   - Cream the butter and brown sugar until light and fluffy. Add the eggs one at a time, beating well after each addition.
3. **Combine Ingredients**:
   - Gradually add the flour mixture to the creamed butter, mixing until just combined. Fold in the soaked fruit mixture along with any remaining liquid, then gently fold in the nuts.
4. **Bake**:
   - Pour the batter into the prepared pan, smoothing the top. Bake for 1.5 to 2 hours, or until a toothpick inserted into the center comes out clean.
   - Once baked, let the cake cool in the pan for 10 minutes, then remove and place it on a wire rack to cool completely.
5. **Finish and Store**:
   - Brush the cake with additional rum or brandy. Wrap it tightly in parchment paper, followed by aluminum foil, and store it in an airtight container.
   - For the best flavor, let the cake age for 2-4 weeks, brushing with rum or brandy weekly.

The classic Christmas fruitcake is a rich, flavorful cake that only improves with time. It makes a wonderful gift or a special treat to serve with a cup of tea during the holidays.

Gingerbread Cake with Cream Cheese Frosting

This gingerbread cake is a moist, spicy cake that fills the kitchen with warm, festive aromas as it bakes. Topped with a tangy cream cheese frosting, this cake combines ginger, molasses, and spices to create a comforting holiday favorite.

Ingredients:

- **Cake Batter**:
    - 2 cups all-purpose flour
    - 1 tsp baking powder
    - 1/2 tsp baking soda
    - 1/2 tsp salt
    - 1 tsp ground ginger
    - 1 tsp ground cinnamon
    - 1/4 tsp ground nutmeg
    - 1/4 tsp ground cloves
    - 1/2 cup unsalted butter, melted
    - 3/4 cup brown sugar
    - 1 cup molasses
    - 1/2 cup buttermilk
    - 2 large eggs, room temperature
    - 1 tsp vanilla extract
- **Cream Cheese Frosting**:
    - 8 oz cream cheese, room temperature
    - 4 tbsp unsalted butter, room temperature

28

- o   2 cups powdered sugar
- o   1 tsp vanilla extract

Instructions:

1. **Prepare the Cake Batter**:
   - o   Preheat your oven to 350°F (175°C). Grease and flour a 9-inch square baking pan.
   - o   In a large mixing bowl, whisk together the flour, baking powder, baking soda, salt, ginger, cinnamon, nutmeg, and cloves.
   - o   In another bowl, combine the melted butter, brown sugar, molasses, buttermilk, eggs, and vanilla extract. Mix until smooth.
2. **Combine Ingredients and Bake**:
   - o   Gradually add the wet ingredients to the dry ingredients, stirring until just combined.
   - o   Pour the batter into the prepared pan and smooth the top. Bake for 35-40 minutes, or until a toothpick inserted into the center comes out clean.
   - o   Let the cake cool in the pan for 10 minutes, then transfer to a wire rack to cool completely.
3. **Make the Frosting**:
   - o   In a medium bowl, beat the cream cheese and butter until smooth and creamy. Gradually add the powdered sugar, beating until fluffy. Mix in the vanilla extract.
4. **Assemble**:
   - o   Once the cake is completely cool, spread the cream cheese frosting over the top. Garnish with a sprinkle of cinnamon or a few pieces of crystallized ginger for a decorative touch.

This gingerbread cake with cream cheese frosting is a cozy, nostalgic treat that's perfect for serving after a holiday meal or at festive gatherings.

Eggnog Bundt Cake

Eggnog bundt cake is a fluffy, flavorful cake that combines the creamy taste of eggnog with warm spices. This festive cake is ideal for eggnog lovers and makes a stunning centerpiece on any holiday dessert table.

Ingredients:

- **Cake Batter:**
    o 3 cups all-purpose flour
    o 2 tsp baking powder
    o 1/2 tsp baking soda
    o 1/2 tsp salt
    o 1/2 tsp ground nutmeg
    o 1 cup unsalted butter, room temperature
    o 1 3/4 cups granulated sugar
    o 4 large eggs, room temperature
    o 1 tsp vanilla extract
    o 1/2 tsp rum extract (optional)
    o 1 1/4 cups eggnog
- **Eggnog Glaze:**
    o 1 cup powdered sugar
    o 2-3 tbsp eggnog
    o A pinch of nutmeg

Instructions:

1. **Prepare the Cake Batter**:
   - Preheat your oven to 350°F (175°C). Grease and flour a bundt pan.
   - In a medium bowl, whisk together the flour, baking powder, baking soda, salt, and nutmeg.
   - In a large bowl, cream the butter and sugar until light and fluffy. Add the eggs one at a time, beating well after each addition. Mix in the vanilla and rum extracts.
2. **Combine Ingredients and Bake**:
   - Alternate adding the dry ingredients and eggnog to the creamed mixture, beginning and ending with the dry ingredients. Mix until just combined.
   - Pour the batter into the prepared bundt pan and smooth the top. Bake for 45-50 minutes, or until a toothpick inserted into the center comes out clean.
   - Let the cake cool in the pan for 15 minutes, then invert onto a wire rack to cool completely.
3. **Prepare the Glaze**:
   - In a small bowl, whisk together the powdered sugar and eggnog until smooth and pourable. Adjust with more eggnog or sugar as needed to reach desired consistency.
4. **Assemble**:
   - Drizzle the glaze over the cooled cake, letting it drip down the sides. Sprinkle with a light dusting of nutmeg for a festive touch.

Eggnog bundt cake is light, fluffy, and full of holiday cheer. It pairs wonderfully with a warm cup of coffee or a glass of eggnog, making it an instant holiday favorite.

Red Velvet Christmas Cake

The Red Velvet Cake is a timeless dessert that has become a holiday favorite thanks to its vibrant color and rich, tangy cream cheese frosting. This cake's deep red hue brings festive cheer, while its tender, velvety crumb and unique cocoa flavor make it both elegant and indulgent. Perfect as a centerpiece dessert, this cake is sure to impress at any Christmas gathering.

Ingredients:

- **Cake Batter**:
    - 2 1/2 cups all-purpose flour
    - 1 1/2 cups granulated sugar
    - 1 tsp baking soda
    - 1 tsp salt
    - 1 tbsp unsweetened cocoa powder
    - 1 1/2 cups vegetable oil
    - 1 cup buttermilk, room temperature
    - 2 large eggs, room temperature
    - 2 tbsp red food coloring
    - 1 tsp vanilla extract
    - 1 tsp white vinegar
- **Cream Cheese Frosting**:
    - 16 oz cream cheese, softened
    - 1 cup unsalted butter, softened
    - 4 cups powdered sugar
    - 1 tsp vanilla extract
    - Optional: A dash of edible glitter or Christmas-themed sprinkles for decoration

Instructions:

1. **Prepare the Cake Batter**:

- o Preheat your oven to 350°F (175°C). Grease and flour two 9-inch round cake pans, or line them with parchment paper.
- o In a large mixing bowl, whisk together the flour, sugar, baking soda, salt, and cocoa powder.
- o In another bowl, mix together the oil, buttermilk, eggs, food coloring, vanilla, and vinegar. Beat until the mixture is smooth and the red color is evenly distributed.

2. **Combine and Bake**:
   - o Gradually add the wet ingredients to the dry ingredients, mixing until just combined. Avoid overmixing, as this can make the cake tough.
   - o Divide the batter evenly between the prepared pans and bake for 25-30 minutes, or until a toothpick inserted in the center comes out clean.
   - o Allow the cakes to cool in their pans for 10 minutes, then turn them out onto wire racks to cool completely.

3. **Make the Cream Cheese Frosting**:
   - o In a large bowl, beat the cream cheese and butter together until smooth and creamy. Gradually add the powdered sugar, one cup at a time, mixing until fluffy. Stir in the vanilla extract.
   - o For extra stability, refrigerate the frosting for 10-15 minutes before applying it to the cake.

4. **Assemble the Cake**:
   - o Place one cake layer on a serving plate and spread a layer of frosting on top. Place the second layer on top and frost the entire cake.
   - o For a festive touch, decorate the top with edible glitter, holiday sprinkles, or small decorative elements like sugar snowflakes or holly berries.

5. **Storage**:

- o Store the cake in the refrigerator, as the cream cheese frosting needs to stay chilled. Before serving, let the cake sit at room temperature for 20-30 minutes to bring out its flavors.

The Red Velvet Christmas Cake is a showstopper that looks as good as it tastes. Its striking color, tender crumb, and rich cream cheese frosting make it a favorite for holiday gatherings, and it's sure to add a pop of festive color to any dessert table.

Chocolate Yule Log (Bûche de Noël)

The Chocolate Yule Log is a classic Christmas dessert that traces back to 19th-century France. Modeled after the Yule log traditionally burned in fireplaces, this cake is made of a soft chocolate sponge rolled with creamy filling and decorated to resemble a log. Topped with ganache and often adorned with "mushrooms" made of meringue or other edible decorations, it brings a whimsical, wintry forest touch to the holiday table.

Ingredients:

- **Chocolate Sponge Cake**:
  - o 3/4 cup all-purpose flour
  - o 1/4 cup cocoa powder
  - o 1 tsp baking powder
  - o 1/4 tsp salt
  - o 4 large eggs, room temperature
  - o 3/4 cup granulated sugar
  - o 1 tsp vanilla extract
- **Filling**:
  - o 1 cup heavy cream, chilled

34

- o   2 tbsp powdered sugar
- o   1 tsp vanilla extract
- **Chocolate Ganache Frosting**:
  - o   1 cup heavy cream
  - o   8 oz semi-sweet chocolate, finely chopped
- **Decorations** (optional):
  - o   Powdered sugar for dusting (to resemble snow)
  - o   Meringue mushrooms or chocolate shavings for a woodsy look
  - o   Fresh rosemary sprigs or cranberries to add a festive, natural touch

Instructions:

1. **Prepare the Sponge Cake**:
   - o   Preheat your oven to 350°F (175°C). Grease a 15x10-inch jelly roll pan and line it with parchment paper, leaving extra parchment on the edges for easy removal.
   - o   In a bowl, sift together the flour, cocoa powder, baking powder, and salt.
   - o   In a separate large mixing bowl, beat the eggs and sugar on high speed for about 5 minutes until the mixture is thick and pale. Add the vanilla extract and mix again.
   - o   Gradually fold the dry ingredients into the egg mixture, being careful not to overmix.
   - o   Spread the batter evenly into the prepared pan and smooth the top with a spatula. Bake for 10-12 minutes, or until the cake springs back when lightly touched.
2. **Roll the Cake**:
   - o   As soon as the cake is out of the oven, turn it out onto a clean kitchen towel dusted with powdered sugar.

Peel off the parchment paper, then gently roll the warm cake up in the towel from the short end. Let it cool completely in the towel to maintain its shape.

3. **Make the Filling**:
   o In a medium bowl, beat the heavy cream, powdered sugar, and vanilla extract until stiff peaks form. This whipped cream filling will be soft and light, adding a creamy contrast to the chocolate.

4. **Assemble the Yule Log**:
   o Carefully unroll the cooled cake and spread the whipped cream filling evenly over the surface, leaving a small border around the edges. Gently roll the cake back up (without the towel), taking care not to press too hard so the filling doesn't spill out.
   o Place the rolled cake seam-side down on a serving platter.

5. **Prepare the Chocolate Ganache Frosting**:
   o In a small saucepan, heat the heavy cream until it just begins to simmer. Pour it over the chopped chocolate and let sit for 2 minutes, then stir until smooth.
   o Allow the ganache to cool until it's thick enough to spread
   o Then cover the outside of the cake with ganache, using a spatula to create a bark-like texture.

6. **Decorate the Yule Log**:
   o Dust with powdered sugar for a snowy effect, and add optional decorations such as meringue mushrooms, chocolate shavings, fresh rosemary, or cranberries to resemble a log in a winter forest.

7. **Serve and Store**:
   o Refrigerate the cake until ready to serve. This cake can be made a day in advance, as it keeps well in the fridge.

The Chocolate Yule Log is both a dessert and a work of art. With its rich chocolate flavor, light filling, and festive appearance, this cake will delight children and adults alike. It's a wonderful choice for a memorable holiday dessert that captures the cozy, rustic charm of the season.

Each of these cakes has its own distinct charm, and together they offer variety and a sense of tradition for Christmas celebrations. Whether you're looking for the elegance of red velvet or the classic look of a chocolate log, these cakes are sure to be a hit at your holiday gatherings.

Chapter 4: Holiday Cookies

Christmas cookies are essential to holiday baking, whether for decorating with loved ones, making homemade gifts, or adding variety to dessert tables. From spiced gingerbread to buttery, melt-in-your-mouth snowballs, these classic cookies will add joy and warmth to your holiday season.

Traditional Gingerbread Men

Gingerbread men are iconic holiday cookies, recognizable by their warm spices and adorable decorations. These cookies are spiced with ginger, cinnamon, and cloves, giving them a rich, holiday flavor and a slightly crisp texture. Decorating gingerbread men is a fun activity for both kids and adults, allowing everyone to create their own unique holiday characters.

Ingredients:

- **Gingerbread Dough**:
    - 3 1/4 cups all-purpose flour
    - 3/4 cup dark brown sugar, packed
    - 1 tbsp ground ginger
    - 1 tbsp ground cinnamon
    - 1/2 tsp ground cloves
    - 1/2 tsp salt
    - 3/4 tsp baking soda
    - 3/4 cup unsalted butter, softened
    - 3/4 cup molasses
    - 1 large egg, room temperature
- **Decorating Icing**:
    - 1 1/2 cups powdered sugar
    - 1-2 tbsp milk or water
    - Food coloring (optional)
    - Candy decorations, such as mini chocolate chips, sprinkles, or red hots

Instructions:

1. **Prepare the Gingerbread Dough**:

- o In a large mixing bowl, whisk together the flour, brown sugar, ginger, cinnamon, cloves, salt, and baking soda.
- o In a separate bowl, beat the butter until creamy, then add the molasses and egg, mixing until smooth. Gradually add the dry ingredients to the wet mixture, mixing until a thick dough forms.
- o Divide the dough in half, shape each half into a disk, wrap in plastic wrap, and refrigerate for at least 1 hour (or up to overnight). Chilling makes the dough easier to roll and helps prevent the cookies from spreading during baking.

2. **Roll and Cut the Dough**:
   - o Preheat your oven to 350°F (175°C) and line baking sheets with parchment paper.
   - o On a lightly floured surface, roll the dough out to about 1/4 inch thickness. Cut out gingerbread men shapes using a cookie cutter, and transfer them to the prepared baking sheets, spacing them about 1 inch apart.

3. **Bake**:
   - o Bake for 8-10 minutes, or until the edges are slightly firm. Be careful not to overbake, as they will continue to firm up as they cool.
   - o Allow the cookies to cool on the baking sheet for 5 minutes, then transfer to a wire rack to cool completely.

4. **Decorate**:
   - o In a small bowl, mix the powdered sugar with milk or water to create a thick icing. Divide into separate bowls and add food coloring as desired.
   - o Use piping bags or zip-top bags with the tip snipped off to pipe faces, buttons, and clothing onto the

gingerbread men. Add candy decorations while the icing is still wet, so they stick.

Gingerbread men are perfect for decorating parties and cookie exchanges. Their warm, spiced flavor is a quintessential taste of the holidays, and their playful appearance brings cheer to any gathering.

Sugar Cookies with Royal Icing

Sugar cookies are known for their versatility and delicate, buttery flavor. With the right dough, they hold their shape beautifully and can be cut into any festive design. Decorated with royal icing, they make a stunning addition to any holiday cookie platter.

Ingredients:

- **Sugar Cookie Dough**:
  - 3 cups all-purpose flour
  - 1 tsp baking powder
  - 1/2 tsp salt
  - 1 cup unsalted butter, softened
  - 1 cup granulated sugar
  - 1 large egg, room temperature
  - 1 1/2 tsp vanilla extract
  - 1/2 tsp almond extract (optional, for added flavor)
- **Royal Icing**:
  - 3 cups powdered sugar
  - 2 tbsp meringue powder (or 2 egg whites if meringue powder isn't available)
  - 5-6 tbsp water
  - Food coloring (optional)
  - Sprinkles, edible glitter, or other decorative elements

Instructions:

1. **Prepare the Sugar Cookie Dough**:
   - In a large bowl, whisk together the flour, baking powder, and salt.
   - In a separate bowl, cream the butter and sugar until light and fluffy. Add the egg, vanilla extract, and almond extract (if using), mixing well.
   - Gradually add the dry ingredients to the wet mixture, mixing until the dough comes together.
   - Divide the dough in half, shape into disks, wrap in plastic wrap, and refrigerate for at least 1 hour (or up to overnight).

2. **Roll and Cut the Dough**:
   - Preheat your oven to 350°F (175°C) and line baking sheets with parchment paper.
   - Roll out the dough on a lightly floured surface to about 1/4 inch thickness. Cut out shapes with holiday cookie cutters and place them on the prepared baking sheets.

3. **Bake**:
   - Bake for 8-10 minutes, or until the edges are just beginning to turn golden. Allow the cookies to cool on the baking sheet for 5 minutes, then transfer to a wire rack to cool completely.

4. **Make the Royal Icing**:
   - In a mixing bowl, beat the powdered sugar, meringue powder, and water on medium speed until the icing holds stiff peaks, about 4-5 minutes. If using egg whites, beat until thick and glossy.
   - Divide the icing into bowls, adding food coloring as desired. For piping and outlining, keep the icing thicker; for flooding, thin it with a little more water until it reaches a syrupy consistency.

5. **Decorate the Cookies**:
   - Use piping bags to outline each cookie, then flood the center with icing. Spread with a toothpick to ensure full coverage, and add sprinkles or edible glitter as desired.
   - Allow the icing to set completely (this can take several hours) before stacking or packaging the cookies.

These sugar cookies are customizable and can be as simple or intricate as you like. They're beautiful, buttery, and make wonderful gifts.

Snowball Cookies (Russian Tea Cakes)

Snowball cookies, also known as Russian Tea Cakes or Mexican Wedding Cookies, are tender, buttery cookies that melt in your mouth. Made with ground nuts and rolled in powdered sugar, they resemble little snowballs, adding a festive winter touch to holiday cookie trays.

Ingredients:

- **Cookie Dough**:
  - 1 cup unsalted butter, softened
  - 1/2 cup powdered sugar
  - 2 tsp vanilla extract
  - 2 cups all-purpose flour
  - 1 cup finely chopped nuts (pecans, walnuts, or almonds work well)
  - 1/4 tsp salt
- **Finishing**:
  - 1-1 1/2 cups powdered sugar (for rolling)

Instructions:

1. **Prepare the Cookie Dough**:
   - Preheat your oven to 350°F (175°C) and line baking sheets with parchment paper.
   - In a large bowl, cream the butter and powdered sugar together until light and fluffy. Add the vanilla extract and mix well.
   - Gradually add the flour, salt, and chopped nuts, mixing until just combined. The dough will be stiff.
2. **Form the Cookies**:
   - Scoop out tablespoon-sized portions of dough and roll them into small balls. Place the balls on the prepared baking sheets, spacing them about 1 inch apart.
3. **Bake**:
   - Bake for 12-15 minutes, or until the bottoms are lightly golden. Be careful not to overbake, as these cookies should remain light in color.

4. **Roll in Powdered Sugar**:
   - While the cookies are still warm, roll each one in powdered sugar, coating them thoroughly. Place them on a wire rack to cool.
   - Once they're completely cool, roll them in powdered sugar a second time for an extra snowy look.

Snowball cookies are delightfully buttery and nutty, with a delicate crumb that melts in your mouth. Their powdered sugar coating gives them a whimsical, wintry appearance, making them a popular choice for Christmas celebrations.

Chocolate Crinkle Cookies

Chocolate Crinkle Cookies are beloved for their soft, fudgy center and beautiful, crackled appearance. As they bake, the powdered sugar coating splits open, creating a snowy, crinkled effect that makes them look like they're dusted with a fresh layer of winter snow. These cookies are rich and chocolatey, with a texture that is slightly chewy on the outside and decadently soft on the inside.

Ingredients:

- 1 cup all-purpose flour
- 1/2 cup unsweetened cocoa powder
- 1 tsp baking powder
- 1/4 tsp salt
- 1 cup granulated sugar
- 1/4 cup vegetable oil
- 2 large eggs, room temperature
- 1 tsp vanilla extract
- 1/2 cup powdered sugar (for rolling)

Instructions:

1. **Prepare the Dough**:
    - In a medium bowl, whisk together the flour, cocoa powder, baking powder, and salt. Set aside.
    - In a large mixing bowl, combine the granulated sugar and vegetable oil. Mix until smooth. Add the eggs, one at a time, and then add the vanilla extract, mixing well after each addition.
    - Gradually add the dry ingredients to the wet ingredients, stirring until just combined. The dough will be thick and sticky.

- o Cover the dough with plastic wrap and refrigerate for at least 2 hours, or until firm. Chilling the dough helps it retain its shape and prevents the powdered sugar from absorbing into the cookies too quickly.

2. **Shape and Roll**:
   - o Preheat your oven to 350°F (175°C) and line baking sheets with parchment paper.
   - o Place the powdered sugar in a small bowl. Scoop out tablespoon-sized portions of dough and roll them into balls, then generously coat each ball in powdered sugar.

3. **Bake**:
   - o Place the coated dough balls on the prepared baking sheets, spacing them about 2 inches apart.
   - o Bake for 10-12 minutes, or until the edges are set but the centers are still slightly soft. Be careful not to overbake, as the centers should remain fudgy.
   - o Allow the cookies to cool on the baking sheet for 5 minutes, then transfer them to a wire rack to cool completely.

Chocolate Crinkle Cookies are both visually striking and incredibly satisfying for chocolate lovers. Their snowy, crinkled look makes them a perfect addition to holiday cookie trays, and their rich, fudgy flavor ensures they'll be a hit with guests.

Peppermint Thumbprint Cookies

Peppermint Thumbprint Cookies add a refreshing, festive twist to traditional thumbprint cookies. These cookies are buttery and tender, with a delightful peppermint-flavored filling that brings a pop of color and holiday cheer. Topped with crushed candy canes, they

45

offer a fun, minty crunch that pairs perfectly with the buttery cookie base.

Ingredients:

- **Cookie Dough**:
    - 1 cup unsalted butter, softened
    - 1/2 cup granulated sugar
    - 1 large egg yolk, room temperature
    - 1 tsp vanilla extract
    - 1/2 tsp peppermint extract
    - 2 cups all-purpose flour
    - 1/4 tsp salt
- **Peppermint Filling**:
    - 1 cup powdered sugar
    - 1-2 tbsp milk (or as needed to reach desired consistency)
    - 1/2 tsp peppermint extract
    - A few drops of red food coloring (optional)
- **Garnish**:
    - Crushed candy canes or peppermint candies for topping

Instructions:

1. **Prepare the Dough**:
    - In a large mixing bowl, cream the butter and granulated sugar together until light and fluffy. Add the egg yolk, vanilla extract, and peppermint extract, mixing until well combined.
    - Gradually add the flour and salt, mixing until a soft dough forms. If the dough is too sticky to handle, refrigerate it for 15-20 minutes.
2. **Shape the Cookies**:

- o Preheat your oven to 350°F (175°C) and line baking sheets with parchment paper.
- o Roll tablespoon-sized portions of dough into balls and place them on the prepared baking sheets, spacing them about 2 inches apart.
- o Use your thumb or the back of a small spoon to make an indentation in the center of each dough ball. Be careful not to press too hard, as you don't want to crack the edges.

3. **Bake**:
- o Bake the cookies for 10-12 minutes, or until the edges are lightly golden. Remove from the oven and immediately use a spoon to gently press down any indentations that may have puffed up during baking.
- o Allow the cookies to cool on the baking sheet for 5 minutes, then transfer them to a wire rack to cool completely.

4. **Prepare the Peppermint Filling**:
- o In a small bowl, combine the powdered sugar, milk, and peppermint extract. Mix until smooth, adding more milk as needed to reach a thick but spreadable consistency.
- o For a festive touch, add a few drops of red food coloring to create a pink filling.

5. **Fill and Garnish**:
- o Spoon a small amount of the peppermint filling into the indentation of each cooled cookie.
- o Sprinkle crushed candy canes or peppermint candies over the filling for a colorful and crunchy garnish.

Peppermint Thumbprint Cookies are refreshing and festive, making them ideal for holiday gatherings. The buttery cookie base pairs beautifully with the peppermint filling, and the crushed candy cane topping adds a perfect holiday crunch. These cookies are fun to make and a joy to share.

Both Chocolate Crinkle Cookies and Peppermint Thumbprint Cookies add delightful variety to holiday cookie trays. With their rich flavors and beautiful presentation, they capture the spirit of the season and bring joy to any celebration.

Chapter 5: Morning Breads and Pastries

Christmas morning is a special time to gather with loved ones, and a selection of freshly baked breads and pastries is the perfect way to make the occasion even more delightful. From soft and gooey

THE MAGIC OF HOLIDAY BAKING

cinnamon rolls to fruit-studded German stollen and bright, citrusy scones, these recipes are easy to make and even easier to enjoy. Here are three delicious Christmas morning recipes to try.

5.1. Cinnamon Rolls with Cream Cheese Icing

Cinnamon rolls are a warm, comforting treat with soft, fluffy dough, a gooey cinnamon-sugar filling, and a creamy, tangy cream cheese icing. These rolls are best served fresh out of the oven and are an irresistible treat for Christmas morning.

Ingredients:

- **Dough**:
    - 4 cups all-purpose flour
    - 1/4 cup granulated sugar
    - 1 packet (2 1/4 tsp) active dry yeast
    - 1 tsp salt
    - 1 cup whole milk
    - 1/4 cup unsalted butter, softened
    - 2 large eggs, room temperature

- **Cinnamon Filling**:
    - 1/2 cup unsalted butter, softened
    - 1 cup brown sugar, packed
    - 2 tbsp ground cinnamon
- **Cream Cheese Icing**:
    - 4 oz cream cheese, softened
    - 1/4 cup unsalted butter, softened
    - 1 cup powdered sugar
    - 1/2 tsp vanilla extract
    - 1-2 tbsp milk (as needed for consistency)

49

Instructions:

1. **Prepare the Dough**:

   ○ Warm the milk to about 110°F (43°C) and add the yeast. Let it sit for 5-10 minutes, until foamy.

   ○ In a large mixing bowl, combine flour, sugar, and salt. Add the yeast mixture, softened butter, and eggs, then knead until a soft, slightly sticky dough forms. You can use a stand mixer with a dough hook or knead by hand.

   ○ Place the dough in a greased bowl, cover with a kitchen towel, and let it rise in a warm place for 1-1.5 hours, or until doubled in size.

2. **Roll Out and Fill**:

   ○ Punch down the dough and transfer it to a floured surface. Roll the dough into a rectangle about 1/4 inch thick.

   ○ Spread the softened butter over the dough, leaving a small border around the edges. Sprinkle the brown sugar and cinnamon evenly over the buttered dough.

3. **Roll and Slice**:

   ○ Starting from the long edge, roll the dough tightly into a log. Cut into 12 equal slices and arrange them in a greased baking dish.

- o Cover and let rise for another 30-45 minutes, until puffed.

4. **Bake**:

- o Preheat your oven to 350°F (175°C). Bake the cinnamon rolls for 25-30 minutes, or until golden brown.

5. **Prepare the Cream Cheese Icing**:

- o In a mixing bowl, beat the cream cheese, butter, powdered sugar, vanilla, and milk until smooth and creamy.

- o Spread the icing over the warm rolls and serve immediately.

Cinnamon rolls with cream cheese icing are the ultimate indulgence for a special holiday breakfast. Soft, gooey, and topped with a rich icing, they're sure to bring warmth and joy to your Christmas morning.

Stollen (German Christmas Bread)

Stollen is a traditional German Christmas bread filled with dried fruits, nuts, and often marzipan, which adds a sweet, rich flavor. The bread is buttery and slightly sweet, with hints of warm spices and a dusting of powdered sugar on top. Stollen is perfect for serving with coffee or tea on Christmas morning.

Ingredients:

- • **Dough**:

- o 3 3/4 cups all-purpose flour
- o 1 packet (2 1/4 tsp) active dry yeast
- o 3/4 cup whole milk, warmed
- o 1/2 cup granulated sugar
- o 1/2 tsp salt
- o 1/2 tsp ground cinnamon
- o 1/2 cup unsalted butter, softened
- o 1 large egg
- o Zest of 1 lemon

- **Filling**:

  - o 1 cup mixed dried fruit (such as raisins, currants, and dried cherries)
  - o 1/2 cup chopped almonds or hazelnuts
  - o 1/2 tsp almond extract
  - o 1/2 tsp vanilla extract
  - o 1/4 cup rum or orange juice (for soaking fruit)
  - o 7 oz marzipan (optional)

- **Finishing**:

  - o 1/4 cup melted butter
  - o 1 cup powdered sugar, for dusting

Instructions:

1. **Prepare the Filling**:

   - o Soak the dried fruit in rum or orange juice for 1-2 hours, then drain.

2. **Make the Dough**:

- o In a small bowl, dissolve the yeast in warm milk and let it sit for 5-10 minutes, until foamy.

- o In a large mixing bowl, combine flour, sugar, salt, and cinnamon. Add the yeast mixture, softened butter, egg, and lemon zest, mixing until a soft dough forms.

- o Knead in the soaked fruit and chopped nuts until evenly distributed. If using marzipan, roll it into a log and place it in the center of the dough. Fold the dough around the marzipan log.

3. **First Rise**:

- o Place the dough in a greased bowl, cover, and let rise in a warm place for 1-1.5 hours, until doubled in size.

4. **Shape and Bake**:

- o Preheat your oven to 350°F (175°C). Shape the dough into a log and place it on a parchment-lined baking sheet.

- o Bake for 30-40 minutes, or until golden brown and hollow-sounding when tapped on the bottom.

5. **Finishing Touches**:

- o While still warm, brush the Stollen with melted butter and generously dust it with powdered sugar. Repeat the sugar dusting once cooled to give it a snow-like appearance.

Stollen is a festive, flavorful bread that keeps well and makes a beautiful centerpiece on Christmas morning. The combination of fruits, nuts, and spices makes each slice a delightful treat.

Cranberry Orange Scones

Cranberry Orange Scones are a delightful mix of tart cranberries and bright orange zest, with a buttery, tender crumb. These scones are easy to make and perfect for serving warm with a pat of butter or a dollop of cream. Their festive flavors and bright color make them ideal for Christmas breakfast.

Ingredients:

- **Scone Dough**:
    - 2 cups all-purpose flour
    - 1/4 cup granulated sugar
    - 1 tbsp baking powder
    - 1/2 tsp salt
    - 1/2 cup unsalted butter, cold and cubed
    - 1/2 cup fresh cranberries, chopped (or dried cranberries)
    - Zest of 1 large orange
    - 1/2 cup heavy cream
    - 1 large egg
    - 1 tsp vanilla extract

- **Orange Glaze** (optional):

- 1 cup powdered sugar
- 2-3 tbsp fresh orange juice
- Zest of 1 orange

Instructions:

1. **Prepare the Dough**:

   - Preheat your oven to 400°F (200°C) and line a baking sheet with parchment paper.

   - In a large bowl, combine flour, sugar, baking powder, and salt. Cut in the cold butter using a pastry cutter or your hands until the mixture resembles coarse crumbs.

   - Stir in the chopped cranberries and orange zest.

2. **Add Wet Ingredients**:

   - In a small bowl, whisk together the heavy cream, egg, and vanilla extract. Gradually add this mixture to the dry ingredients, stirring until just combined.

3. **Shape and Cut the Scones**:

   - Turn the dough out onto a lightly floured surface and pat it into an 8-inch circle, about 3/4 inch thick. Cut into 8 wedges and place them on the prepared baking sheet.

4. **Bake**:

- Bake for 15-18 minutes, or until the scones are golden brown and a toothpick inserted into the center comes out clean. Allow to cool slightly.

5. **Make the Orange Glaze**:

  - In a small bowl, whisk together powdered sugar, orange juice, and orange zest until smooth. Drizzle the glaze over the warm scones before serving.

Cranberry Orange Scones are a vibrant and refreshing addition to Christmas breakfast. The tartness of the cranberries is balanced by the sweetness of the glaze, and the orange zest gives them a burst of citrusy flavor that's perfect for the holidays.

Holiday Sticky Buns

Holiday Sticky Buns are a beloved breakfast treat with pillowy-soft dough, a gooey caramelized topping, and a comforting mix of cinnamon and brown sugar. Made with chopped pecans or walnuts for a nutty crunch, these sticky buns are ideal for a holiday brunch or breakfast.

Ingredients:

- **Dough**:
  - 4 cups all-purpose flour
  - 1 packet (2 1/4 tsp) active dry yeast
  - 1 cup whole milk, warmed
  - 1/3 cup granulated sugar
  - 1/2 cup unsalted butter, softened
  - 2 large eggs, room temperature

- o   1 tsp salt

- **Filling**:

  - o   1/2 cup unsalted butter, softened
  - o   1 cup brown sugar, packed
  - o   2 tbsp ground cinnamon
  - o   1/2 cup chopped pecans or walnuts (optional)

- **Caramel Topping**:

  - o   3/4 cup unsalted butter
  - o   1 cup brown sugar, packed
  - o   1/4 cup heavy cream
  - o   1/2 cup chopped pecans or walnuts

Instructions:

1. **Prepare the Dough**:

   - o   Warm the milk to around 110°F (43°C) and sprinkle the yeast over it. Let it sit for about 5-10 minutes until it becomes foamy.

   - o   In a large mixing bowl, combine flour, sugar, and salt. Add the yeast mixture, softened butter, and eggs. Knead until a soft, smooth dough forms—about 8-10 minutes if kneading by hand, or 5-6 minutes using a stand mixer with a dough hook.

   - o   Place the dough in a greased bowl, cover, and let it rise in a warm area for about 1-1.5 hours, or until doubled in size.

2. **Make the Caramel Topping**:

- o In a saucepan, melt the butter and brown sugar over medium heat, stirring until smooth. Remove from heat and stir in the heavy cream. Pour this caramel mixture into a greased 9x13-inch baking pan, spreading it evenly.

- o Sprinkle the chopped nuts over the caramel layer.

3. **Fill and Roll the Dough**:

- o Punch down the risen dough and transfer it to a floured surface. Roll the dough into a rectangle about 1/4 inch thick.

- o Spread the softened butter over the dough, then sprinkle with brown sugar and cinnamon. Add the chopped nuts, if desired.

- o Starting from one long edge, roll the dough tightly into a log. Slice the log into 12 equal rolls.

4. **Arrange and Rise Again**:

- o Place the sliced rolls on top of the caramel-nut mixture in the baking pan. Cover and let them rise for another 30-45 minutes until puffy.

5. **Bake**:

- o Preheat your oven to 350°F (175°C) and bake the sticky buns for 30-35 minutes, or until golden brown. Let them cool for a few minutes, then invert the pan onto a serving platter so the gooey caramel topping covers each bun.

Holiday Sticky Buns are best enjoyed warm. The soft, buttery dough, gooey caramel, and crunchy nuts make these buns a delightful indulgence, perfect for Christmas morning or any holiday celebration.

5.5. Chocolate Babka

Chocolate Babka is a stunning, braided bread with layers of rich chocolate filling swirled into a soft, slightly sweet dough. This classic Eastern European bread has become a holiday favorite for its beautiful appearance and irresistible combination of bread and chocolate. Babka can be made with a variety of fillings, but the chocolate version is especially beloved.

Ingredients:

- **Dough**:
    - 4 cups all-purpose flour
    - 1/2 cup granulated sugar
    - 2 1/4 tsp active dry yeast
    - 1 cup whole milk, warmed
    - 1/2 cup unsalted butter, softened
    - 2 large eggs, room temperature
    - 1 tsp salt

- **Chocolate Filling**:
    - 1 cup dark chocolate, chopped (or chocolate chips)
    - 1/4 cup unsalted butter
    - 1/4 cup cocoa powder
    - 1/4 cup powdered sugar

- **Syrup** (for extra sweetness and shine):
    - 1/2 cup water
    - 1/2 cup sugar

Instructions:

1. **Prepare the Dough**:
    - Dissolve the yeast in warmed milk, and let it sit for 5-10 minutes until foamy.

    - In a large mixing bowl, combine flour, sugar, and salt. Add the yeast mixture, softened butter, and eggs. Knead until smooth and elastic, about 8-10 minutes by hand or 5-6 minutes in a stand mixer.

    - Place the dough in a greased bowl, cover, and let it rise in a warm place for 1-1.5 hours, or until doubled in size.

2. **Make the Chocolate Filling**:
    - Melt the chocolate and butter together in a saucepan over low heat or in a microwave-safe bowl, stirring frequently. Once melted, add the cocoa powder and powdered sugar, stirring until smooth. Let the filling cool slightly before spreading it on the dough.

3. **Roll and Fill the Dough**:
    - Punch down the risen dough and transfer it to a lightly floured surface. Roll the dough into a rectangle about 1/4 inch thick.

- o Spread the chocolate filling evenly over the dough, leaving a small border around the edges.

4. **Shape and Braid the Babka**:

   - o Starting from a long edge, roll the dough into a tight log. Cut the log in half lengthwise to expose the chocolate layers.

   - o Twist the two halves around each other, keeping the cut sides facing up, and pinch the ends to seal. Carefully place the twisted babka into a greased 9x5-inch loaf pan.

5. **Second Rise**:

   - o Cover the loaf pan and let the babka rise for another 30-45 minutes until puffy.

6. **Bake and Make the Syrup**:

   - o Preheat your oven to 350°F (175°C) and bake the babka for 30-35 minutes, or until golden brown and cooked through.

   - o While the babka is baking, prepare the syrup by combining the water and sugar in a small saucepan. Bring to a boil and simmer until the sugar dissolves.

7. **Finish and Serve**:

   - o Brush the warm syrup over the babka immediately after it comes out of the oven to give it a glossy, sweet finish. Let the babka cool slightly before slicing and serving.

Chocolate Babka is not only delicious but also visually stunning. The intricate layers of dough and chocolate filling create a beautiful marbled effect, making it a show-stopping centerpiece on any holiday breakfast table. The chocolate filling is rich and decadent, providing a wonderful contrast to the light, fluffy dough.

Both Holiday Sticky Buns and Chocolate Babka are sure to impress on Christmas morning. These recipes bring a special touch to the holiday breakfast table with their warm, comforting flavors and festive presentations. Whether you choose the gooey, nutty goodness of sticky buns or the elegant, chocolate-swirled babka, each of these treats will make the holiday morning even more memorable.

Chapter 6: Chocolates and Candies

Christmas chocolates and candies capture the season's sweetness, adding cheer to gatherings and making thoughtful homemade gifts. With rich, creamy fudge, refreshing peppermint bark, and indulgent chocolate-covered caramels, this chapter explores the joy of festive confections. These treats are designed to impress and are easily customizable with seasonal flavors and festive decorations.

Classic Chocolate Fudge

Chocolate fudge is a smooth, creamy, and decadently rich treat that has become a holiday staple. This classic recipe is easy to make with minimal ingredients, making it perfect for beginner and experienced bakers alike. The dense, melt-in-your-mouth texture of chocolate fudge is ideal for satisfying holiday chocolate cravings.

Ingredients:

- 3 cups semisweet chocolate chips (or dark chocolate chips for a richer taste)
- 1 can (14 oz) sweetened condensed milk
- 1/4 cup unsalted butter, cubed
- 1/2 tsp vanilla extract
- Optional toppings: crushed peppermint, chopped nuts, or sprinkles

Instructions:

1. **Prepare the Pan**:

   o   Line an 8x8-inch baking pan with parchment paper, leaving some overhang for easy removal. Set aside.

2. **Melt the Chocolate Mixture**:

   o   In a medium saucepan, combine the chocolate chips, sweetened condensed milk, and butter over low heat. Stir continuously until the chocolate and butter are completely melted and the mixture is smooth and glossy.

3. **Add Vanilla**:

   o   Remove the saucepan from the heat and stir in the vanilla extract. Mix until well incorporated.

4. **Pour and Smooth**:

   o   Pour the fudge mixture into the prepared baking pan, spreading it evenly. Smooth the top with a spatula. If desired, sprinkle toppings like crushed peppermint, chopped nuts, or festive sprinkles over the fudge.

5. **Chill and Set**:

   o   Refrigerate the fudge for at least 2 hours, or until completely firm. Once set, lift the fudge out of the pan using the parchment paper, and cut into small squares.

6. **Serve and Store**:

   o Store the fudge in an airtight container in the refrigerator for up to two weeks.

Classic Chocolate Fudge is a rich and delightful treat, perfect for serving on a dessert platter or wrapping in holiday-themed boxes for gift-giving. Its smooth texture and customizable toppings make it a versatile favorite during the holiday season.

6.2. Peppermint Bark

Peppermint bark is a festive treat that combines smooth chocolate with crunchy peppermint candy. It's visually striking with its layers of dark and white chocolate, making it as delightful to look at as it is to eat. Peppermint bark is a great holiday recipe to make with kids, and it's always a hit as a gift.

Ingredients:

- 12 oz dark or semisweet chocolate, chopped

- 12 oz white chocolate, chopped

- 1/2 tsp peppermint extract

- 1/2 cup crushed candy canes or peppermint candies

Instructions:

1. **Prepare a Baking Sheet**:

   o Line a baking sheet with parchment paper or aluminum foil to prevent sticking.

2. **Melt the Dark Chocolate**:

- o In a heatproof bowl, melt the dark chocolate using a double boiler or microwave in 20-second intervals, stirring in between until smooth.

- o Stir in 1/4 teaspoon of peppermint extract to add a hint of peppermint flavor to the dark chocolate layer.

3. **Layer the Dark Chocolate:**

- o Pour the melted dark chocolate onto the lined baking sheet, spreading it evenly with a spatula. Place the sheet in the refrigerator for about 15-20 minutes, allowing the dark chocolate layer to partially set.

4. **Melt the White Chocolate:**

- o While the dark chocolate is setting, melt the white chocolate in a similar manner.

- o Add the remaining 1/4 teaspoon of peppermint extract to the white chocolate for a more pronounced peppermint flavor.

5. **Layer the White Chocolate:**

- o Carefully spread the melted white chocolate over the partially set dark chocolate layer, spreading it evenly to cover the surface.

6. **Add Crushed Peppermint:**

- o Sprinkle the crushed candy canes or peppermint candies over the white chocolate while it is still warm. Gently press down on the candy to ensure it adheres to the chocolate.

7. **Chill and Break:**

- o Refrigerate the bark for about 30 minutes, or until fully set. Once hardened, break the peppermint bark into irregular pieces.

8. **Serve and Store**:

   - o Store the peppermint bark in an airtight container at room temperature for up to two weeks.

Peppermint bark is a classic holiday treat that brings a refreshing crunch to chocolate lovers. Its festive appearance and simple preparation make it an excellent addition to any holiday dessert platter or as a handmade gift.

Chocolate-Covered Caramels

Chocolate-covered caramels are the ultimate holiday indulgence, featuring a chewy caramel center encased in smooth chocolate. These treats are a perfect mix of textures, with the softness of caramel and the snap of chocolate. They can be decorated with a sprinkle of sea salt or holiday sprinkles for added flavor and flair.

Ingredients:

- **Caramel**:

  - o 1 cup heavy cream
  - o 1/2 cup unsalted butter, cubed
  - o 1 1/2 cups granulated sugar
  - o 1/4 cup light corn syrup
  - o 1/4 cup water
  - o 1/2 tsp vanilla extract
  - o Optional: flaky sea salt for garnish

- **Chocolate Coating**:
  - 12 oz dark or milk chocolate, chopped
  - Optional toppings: holiday sprinkles, crushed nuts, or more sea salt

Instructions:

1. **Prepare the Pan**:
   - Line an 8x8-inch baking dish with parchment paper and lightly grease it with butter.

2. **Make the Caramel**:
   - In a medium saucepan, combine the heavy cream and butter. Heat over medium-low heat until the butter melts, then remove from heat and set aside.

   - In a separate large saucepan, combine sugar, corn syrup, and water. Cook over medium-high heat, stirring until the sugar dissolves. Continue to cook without stirring until the mixture turns a deep amber color, about 10-12 minutes.

   - Carefully pour the warm cream mixture into the caramel (it will bubble up). Stir gently until fully combined and smooth. Continue cooking the caramel until it reaches 245°F (118°C) on a candy thermometer, then remove from heat and stir in the vanilla extract.

3. **Pour and Set**:

o   Pour the caramel into the prepared pan and let it sit at room temperature until firm, about 1-2 hours.

4. **Cut the Caramel**:

o   Once the caramel is firm, lift it out of the pan using the parchment paper and cut it into small squares or rectangles.

5. **Melt the Chocolate**:

o   Melt the chocolate in a heatproof bowl over a double boiler or in the microwave in 20-second intervals, stirring in between until smooth.

6. **Dip the Caramels**:

o   Using a fork or candy dipping tool, dip each caramel square into the melted chocolate, allowing any excess chocolate to drip off. Place the chocolate-covered caramels on a parchment-lined baking sheet.

7. **Add Garnishes**:

o   While the chocolate is still wet, sprinkle a pinch of flaky sea salt or add festive sprinkles on top of each caramel for decoration.

8. **Set and Store**:

o   Let the caramels set at room temperature or in the refrigerator. Store them in an airtight container in a cool, dry place for up to two weeks.

Chocolate-covered caramels offer a chewy, chocolatey experience that's sure to impress friends and family. These caramels make a delightful homemade gift or can be served as an indulgent treat for holiday guests.

Peppermint Bark

Peppermint bark is a festive treat that combines smooth chocolate with crunchy peppermint candy. It's visually striking with its layers of dark and white chocolate, making it as delightful to look at as it is to eat. Peppermint bark is a great holiday recipe to make with kids, and it's always a hit as a gift.

Ingredients:

- 12 oz dark or semisweet chocolate, chopped
- 12 oz white chocolate, chopped
- 1/2 tsp peppermint extract
- 1/2 cup crushed candy canes or peppermint candies

Instructions:

1. **Prepare a Baking Sheet**:
   o Line a baking sheet with parchment paper or aluminum foil to prevent sticking.
2. **Melt the Dark Chocolate**:
   o In a heatproof bowl, melt the dark chocolate using a double boiler or microwave in 20-second intervals, stirring in between until smooth.
   o Stir in 1/4 teaspoon of peppermint extract to add a hint of peppermint flavor to the dark chocolate layer.
3. **Layer the Dark Chocolate**:

70

- o   Pour the melted dark chocolate onto the lined baking sheet, spreading it evenly with a spatula. Place the sheet in the refrigerator for about 15-20 minutes, allowing the dark chocolate layer to partially set.

4. **Melt the White Chocolate**:
   - o   While the dark chocolate is setting, melt the white chocolate in a similar manner.
   - o   Add the remaining 1/4 teaspoon of peppermint extract to the white chocolate for a more pronounced peppermint flavor.

5. **Layer the White Chocolate**:
   - o   Carefully spread the melted white chocolate over the partially set dark chocolate layer, spreading it evenly to cover the surface.

6. **Add Crushed Peppermint**:
   - o   Sprinkle the crushed candy canes or peppermint candies over the white chocolate while it is still warm. Gently press down on the candy to ensure it adheres to the chocolate.

7. **Chill and Break**:
   - o   Refrigerate the bark for about 30 minutes, or until fully set. Once hardened, break the peppermint bark into irregular pieces.

8. **Serve and Store**:
   - o   Store the peppermint bark in an airtight container at room temperature for up to two weeks.

Peppermint bark is a classic holiday treat that brings a refreshing crunch to chocolate lovers. Its festive appearance and simple preparation make it an excellent addition to any holiday dessert platter or as a handmade gift.

Chocolate-Covered Caramels

Chocolate-covered caramels are the ultimate holiday indulgence, featuring a chewy caramel center encased in smooth chocolate. These treats are a perfect mix of textures, with the softness of caramel and the snap of chocolate. They can be decorated with a sprinkle of sea salt or holiday sprinkles for added flavor and flair.

Ingredients:

- **Caramel**:
    o 1 cup heavy cream
    o 1/2 cup unsalted butter, cubed
    o 1 1/2 cups granulated sugar
    o 1/4 cup light corn syrup
    o 1/4 cup water
    o 1/2 tsp vanilla extract
    o Optional: flaky sea salt for garnish
- **Chocolate Coating**:
    o 12 oz dark or milk chocolate, chopped
    o Optional toppings: holiday sprinkles, crushed nuts, or more sea salt

Instructions:

1. **Prepare the Pan**:
    o Line an 8x8-inch baking dish with parchment paper and lightly grease it with butter.
2. **Make the Caramel**:
    o In a medium saucepan, combine the heavy cream and butter. Heat over medium-low heat until the butter melts, then remove from heat and set aside.
    o In a separate large saucepan, combine sugar, corn syrup, and water. Cook over medium-high heat,

72

stirring until the sugar dissolves. Continue to cook without stirring until the mixture turns a deep amber color, about 10-12 minutes.

- o Carefully pour the warm cream mixture into the caramel (it will bubble up). Stir gently until fully combined and smooth. Continue cooking the caramel until it reaches 245°F (118°C) on a candy thermometer, then remove from heat and stir in the vanilla extract.

3. **Pour and Set**:
   - o Pour the caramel into the prepared pan and let it sit at room temperature until firm, about 1-2 hours.

4. **Cut the Caramel**:
   - o Once the caramel is firm, lift it out of the pan using the parchment paper and cut it into small squares or rectangles.

5. **Melt the Chocolate**:
   - o Melt the chocolate in a heatproof bowl over a double boiler or in the microwave in 20-second intervals, stirring in between until smooth.

6. **Dip the Caramels**:
   - o Using a fork or candy dipping tool, dip each caramel square into the melted chocolate, allowing any excess chocolate to drip off. Place the chocolate-covered caramels on a parchment-lined baking sheet.

7. **Add Garnishes**:
   - o While the chocolate is still wet, sprinkle a pinch of flaky sea salt or add festive sprinkles on top of each caramel for decoration.

8. **Set and Store**:
   - o Let the caramels set at room temperature or in the refrigerator. Store them in an airtight container in a cool, dry place for up to two weeks.

Chocolate-covered caramels offer a chewy, chocolatey experience that's sure to impress friends and family. These caramels make a delightful homemade gift or can be served as an indulgent treat for holiday guests.

Each of these recipes—Classic Chocolate Fudge, Peppermint Bark, and Chocolate-Covered Caramels—brings unique textures and flavors to a holiday dessert spread. These confections are easily packaged as gifts, bringing joy and a taste of the season to everyone on your list. Whether you make just one or all three, these holiday chocolates and candies are sure to be a hit with family and friends.

Truffles with Holiday Spices

Truffles are luxurious, bite-sized chocolates with a creamy ganache center. This recipe elevates the classic chocolate truffle by incorporating holiday spices, creating a warming, festive flavor profile. With hints of cinnamon, nutmeg, and cloves, these truffles are perfect for anyone looking to add a sophisticated, seasonal touch to their holiday treats.

Ingredients:

- **Ganache Filling**:
    - 8 oz high-quality dark chocolate, finely chopped
    - 1/2 cup heavy cream
    - 1/4 tsp cinnamon
    - 1/8 tsp ground nutmeg
    - 1/8 tsp ground cloves
    - 1/4 tsp ground ginger
    - 1/2 tsp vanilla extract
    - Optional: pinch of cayenne pepper for a subtle kick

- **Coating Options**:
  - Cocoa powder
  - Finely chopped nuts (e.g., hazelnuts, almonds, or pecans)
  - Powdered sugar mixed with a pinch of cinnamon
  - Crushed candy canes for a peppermint crunch

Instructions:

1. **Prepare the Ganache**:
   - Place the chopped chocolate in a heatproof bowl.
   - In a small saucepan, heat the heavy cream over medium heat until it just begins to simmer—do not let it boil.
   - Pour the hot cream over the chocolate and let it sit for 2-3 minutes. Then, stir until the chocolate is completely melted and smooth.
2. **Add Holiday Spices**:
   - Once the chocolate is fully melted and smooth, add the cinnamon, nutmeg, cloves, ginger, vanilla extract, and cayenne pepper if using. Stir until all the spices are evenly incorporated.
   - Cover the bowl with plastic wrap and refrigerate the ganache for about 1-2 hours, or until it is firm enough to shape.
3. **Shape the Truffles**:
   - Once the ganache is firm, use a small cookie scoop or teaspoon to scoop out portions of the chocolate. Roll each portion into a smooth ball between the palms of your hands.
4. **Coat the Truffles**:

- o Roll each truffle in your choice of coating. Cocoa powder adds a classic look, while crushed nuts or candy canes add texture and flavor. Alternatively, a mix of cinnamon and powdered sugar adds a sweet, spiced finish.
- o Place the coated truffles on a parchment-lined baking sheet.

5. **Chill and Serve**:
   - o Refrigerate the truffles for about 30 minutes to firm up the coating. Store them in an airtight container in the refrigerator, where they'll keep for up to 2 weeks.

Truffles with Holiday Spices are indulgent and full of flavor, making them a perfect treat to enjoy by the fire or to give as elegant gifts. Their velvety texture and aromatic spices make these truffles a memorable addition to any holiday dessert spread.

Homemade Marshmallows

Homemade marshmallows are a fun, festive treat that's surprisingly easy to make. Fluffy, soft, and delightfully sweet, they add a special touch to hot chocolate, holiday s'mores, or dessert platters. While classic vanilla-flavored marshmallows are always a hit, you can easily customize them with holiday flavors like peppermint or cinnamon to suit the season.

Ingredients:

- **Marshmallow Base:**
  - o 3 packets (about 7.5 tsp) unflavored gelatin
  - o 1 cup cold water, divided
  - o 1 1/2 cups granulated sugar

76

- o   1 cup light corn syrup
- o   1/4 tsp salt
- o   1 tbsp vanilla extract or peppermint extract (for peppermint-flavored marshmallows)
- o   Optional: red food coloring for a swirl effect (especially fun with peppermint flavor)

- **Coating**:
  - o   1/4 cup powdered sugar
  - o   1/4 cup cornstarch

Instructions:

1. **Prepare the Pan**:
   - o   Grease a 9x13-inch baking pan and line it with parchment paper. Lightly grease the parchment paper to ensure the marshmallows don't stick.
2. **Bloom the Gelatin**:
   - o   In the bowl of a stand mixer, sprinkle the gelatin over 1/2 cup of cold water. Let it sit for about 5-10 minutes until the gelatin has absorbed the water and become slightly thickened.
3. **Make the Syrup**:
   - o   In a medium saucepan, combine the remaining 1/2 cup of cold water, granulated sugar, corn syrup, and salt. Heat over medium-high heat, stirring until the sugar dissolves.
   - o   Attach a candy thermometer to the side of the pan and continue to cook the mixture without stirring until

it reaches 240°F (116°C). Remove the saucepan from heat immediately.

4. **Combine and Whip**:
   o With the stand mixer on low speed, carefully pour the hot syrup into the bloomed gelatin. Once all the syrup is added, increase the mixer speed to high and whip for 10-12 minutes, or until the mixture becomes thick, glossy, and lukewarm.
   o Add the vanilla or peppermint extract in the final minute of mixing. If you want a peppermint swirl, add a few drops of red food coloring and gently fold it in to create a marbled effect.

5. **Pour and Set**:
   o Pour the marshmallow mixture into the prepared pan, using a spatula to spread it evenly.
   o Dust the top with a mixture of powdered sugar and cornstarch. Let the marshmallows sit uncovered at room temperature for at least 4 hours, or overnight, to set completely.

6. **Cut and Coat**:
   o Once set, lift the marshmallow slab out of the pan using the parchment paper. Dust a sharp knife with the powdered sugar and cornstarch mixture, then cut the marshmallows into squares.
   o Toss the cut marshmallows in the remaining powdered sugar and cornstarch to prevent sticking.

7. **Serve and Store**:
   o Store homemade marshmallows in an airtight container at room temperature for up to 2 weeks. They're perfect for hot chocolate, dessert platters, or as a special holiday gift.

Homemade Marshmallows are light and fluffy, with a melt-in-your-mouth texture that's far superior to store-bought versions.

78

Customizing them with seasonal flavors like peppermint makes them especially festive, and their versatility makes them a great addition to any holiday menu.

Truffles with Holiday Spices and Homemade Marshmallows are both delightful treats that elevate any holiday gathering. The truffles bring warmth and richness with their spiced ganache, while the marshmallows add a light, sweet touch that pairs perfectly with other Christmas desserts. Both treats make thoughtful, handmade gifts and are bound to bring smiles to anyone who receive

Chapter 7: Ice Creams And Frozen Treats

Holiday ice creams and frozen treats offer a unique way to enjoy classic holiday flavors. They're perfect for festive gatherings, offering a modern twist on Christmas classics in the form of chilled, creamy delights. This chapter explores three standout frozen desserts that are easy to make at home and sure to impress guests and family alike.

Eggnog Ice Cream

Eggnog Ice Cream combines the creamy, spiced richness of eggnog with the smooth texture of ice cream, making it a perfect holiday dessert. With hints of nutmeg, cinnamon, and a dash of rum or bourbon, this ice cream captures the warmth of traditional eggnog in a refreshingly cool format.

Ingredients:

- 1 1/2 cups whole milk
- 1 1/2 cups heavy cream

- 1 cup granulated sugar
- 6 large egg yolks
- 1/2 tsp vanilla extract
- 1/4 tsp freshly grated nutmeg (plus extra for garnish)
- 1/4 tsp ground cinnamon
- 2 tbsp rum or bourbon (optional, for an adult version)

Instructions:

1. **Prepare the Base**:
   - In a medium saucepan, combine the milk, heavy cream, and half of the sugar. Heat over medium heat until the mixture begins to steam, but do not let it boil.
2. **Whisk the Egg Yolks**:
   - In a separate bowl, whisk together the egg yolks and the remaining sugar until the mixture is pale and slightly thickened.
3. **Temper the Eggs**:
   - Slowly pour a ladleful of the hot milk mixture into the egg yolk mixture, whisking constantly to prevent the eggs from curdling. Gradually add the rest of the hot milk mixture, whisking as you go.
4. **Cook the Custard**:
   - Pour the egg and milk mixture back into the saucepan and cook over medium heat, stirring constantly with a wooden spoon or heatproof spatula. Continue cooking

until the mixture thickens and coats the back of the spoon, about 170°F (77°C).

5. **Add Flavorings**:
   - ○ Remove the saucepan from heat and stir in the vanilla extract, nutmeg, cinnamon, and rum or bourbon if desired.
6. **Chill the Mixture**:
   - ○ Pour the custard into a clean bowl and cover with plastic wrap, pressing it directly onto the surface to prevent a skin from forming. Chill the mixture in the refrigerator for at least 4 hours or overnight.
7. **Churn the Ice Cream**:
   - ○ Once chilled, pour the custard into an ice cream maker and churn according to the manufacturer's instructions, usually about 20-25 minutes.
8. **Freeze and Serve**:
   - ○ Transfer the ice cream to an airtight container and freeze for at least 2 hours for a firmer texture. Serve in bowls with an extra sprinkle of nutmeg for garnish.

Eggnog Ice Cream is a creamy, luxurious treat with the comforting flavors of nutmeg and cinnamon. It's perfect for holiday dinners as a refreshing dessert or for creating a unique ice cream sundae bar.

Peppermint Mocha Gelato

Peppermint Mocha Gelato is a refreshing, creamy treat inspired by the classic holiday drink. With a base of rich chocolate, a hint of coffee, and cool peppermint, this gelato brings together three festive flavors in a balanced and delicious way.

Ingredients:

- 2 cups whole milk
- 1 cup heavy cream
- 3/4 cup granulated sugar
- 1/2 cup unsweetened cocoa powder
- 1/4 cup brewed espresso or strong coffee
- 1/2 tsp peppermint extract
- Optional: crushed peppermint candies for garnish

Instructions:

1. **Prepare the Gelato Base**:
   o In a medium saucepan, whisk together the milk, heavy cream, and sugar. Heat over medium heat until the mixture is just about to simmer, but do not let it boil.
2. **Add Cocoa and Espresso**:
   o Whisk in the cocoa powder until fully dissolved, then add the brewed espresso or coffee. Stir until the mixture is smooth and well combined.
3. **Cool and Add Peppermint**:
   o Remove the saucepan from heat and stir in the peppermint extract. Taste and adjust if you'd like a stronger peppermint flavor.
4. **Chill the Mixture**:
   o Pour the gelato mixture into a bowl, cover with plastic wrap, and refrigerate for at least 4 hours or overnight.
5. **Churn the Gelato**:
   o Once chilled, pour the mixture into an ice cream maker and churn according to the manufacturer's instructions.
6. **Freeze and Garnish**:
   o Transfer the gelato to an airtight container and freeze for at least 2 hours to firm up. Before serving, sprinkle with crushed peppermint candies for an extra festive touch.

Peppermint Mocha Gelato is a refreshing holiday dessert that combines chocolate, coffee, and peppermint into a smooth, creamy treat. It's perfect for coffee lovers and makes a delightful end to a holiday meal.

Gingerbread Ice Cream Sandwiches

Gingerbread Ice Cream Sandwiches offer a fun and festive twist on the classic cookie sandwich. With spiced gingerbread cookies and a creamy vanilla or cinnamon ice cream filling, these sandwiches are perfect for holiday gatherings, and kids love making (and eating) them.

Ingredients:

For the Gingerbread Cookies:

- 2 1/4 cups all-purpose flour
- 1 tbsp ground ginger
- 1 tsp ground cinnamon
- 1/2 tsp ground cloves
- 1/4 tsp ground nutmeg
- 1/4 tsp baking soda
- 1/4 tsp salt
- 3/4 cup unsalted butter, softened
- 1/2 cup dark brown sugar
- 1/2 cup molasses
- 1 large egg
- 1 tsp vanilla extract

For the Ice Cream Filling:

- 1 quart vanilla ice cream or cinnamon ice cream, softened

Instructions:

1. **Prepare the Cookie Dough**:
   - In a medium bowl, whisk together the flour, ginger, cinnamon, cloves, nutmeg, baking soda, and salt.
   - In a separate large bowl, beat the butter and brown sugar together until light and fluffy. Add the molasses, egg, and vanilla extract, mixing until smooth.
2. **Combine and Chill**:
   - Gradually add the dry ingredients to the wet ingredients, mixing until a dough forms. Cover the dough and refrigerate for at least 1 hour to make it easier to roll out.
3. **Roll and Cut the Cookies**:
   - Preheat the oven to 350°F (175°C) and line baking sheets with parchment paper.
   - Roll the dough out on a floured surface to about 1/4-inch thickness. Use a round cookie cutter to cut out cookies. Place them on the prepared baking sheets about 1 inch apart.
4. **Bake**:
   - Bake the cookies for 8-10 minutes, or until the edges are just beginning to turn golden. Let them cool on the baking sheets for a few minutes before transferring to a wire rack to cool completely.
5. **Assemble the Ice Cream Sandwiches**:
   - Once the cookies are cool, place a scoop of softened vanilla or cinnamon ice cream on the bottom of one cookie. Gently press a second cookie on top to create a sandwich. Smooth any excess ice cream around the edges.
6. **Freeze to Set**:

- o Place the assembled sandwiches on a baking sheet and freeze for at least 1 hour to firm up. For a festive touch, you can roll the edges of the sandwiches in holiday sprinkles.

Gingerbread Ice Cream Sandwiches combine the warmth of spiced gingerbread cookies with the cool creaminess of ice cream, creating a delightful mix of textures and flavors. They're a fun, hands-on dessert that's perfect for holiday parties.

Cranberry Sorbet

Cranberry Sorbet is a delightful, light dessert that highlights the tangy, fruity flavor of cranberries, making it a perfect palate cleanser or dessert choice for a holiday feast. It's vibrant, refreshing, and beautifully festive with its deep red color, bringing a touch of elegance to the dessert table.

Ingredients:

- 1 1/2 cups fresh or frozen cranberries

- 1 cup water

- 3/4 cup granulated sugar (adjust to taste)

- 1/2 cup fresh orange juice (about 1 large orange)

- 1 tsp orange zest

- 1 tbsp lemon juice

- Optional: 1 tbsp Grand Marnier or orange liqueur (for a more complex flavor and smoother texture)

Instructions:

1. **Make the Cranberry Base**:

    o In a medium saucepan, combine the cranberries, water, and sugar. Bring to a simmer over medium heat, stirring occasionally until the cranberries have burst and softened, about 10 minutes.

    o Remove the saucepan from heat and let the mixture cool slightly.

2. **Blend the Mixture**:

    o Transfer the cranberry mixture to a blender or food processor and add the orange juice, orange zest, and lemon juice. Blend until smooth and combined.

3. **Strain for Smoothness**:

    o For a smoother sorbet, pass the mixture through a fine-mesh sieve to remove any cranberry skins. Press down on the solids to extract as much liquid as possible, then discard the solids.

4. **Add Optional Liqueur**:

    o Stir in the Grand Marnier or orange liqueur if desired. This not only adds a subtle flavor but also helps create a smoother texture.

5. **Chill and Churn**:

○ Cover the mixture and refrigerate for at least 2 hours or until thoroughly chilled. Then, pour the mixture into an ice cream maker and churn according to the manufacturer's instructions, typically about 20 minutes.

6. **Freeze and Serve**:

○ Transfer the churned sorbet to an airtight container and freeze for an additional 1-2 hours to firm up. Serve scoops in small bowls or glasses, garnished with a fresh cranberry or an orange twist if desired.

Cranberry Sorbet is a refreshing, tart dessert that pairs well with rich holiday dishes and offers a festive twist on the usual sorbet flavors. Its bold red color and citrusy tang make it a memorable addition to any holiday menu.

Spiced Hot Chocolate Ice Cream

Spiced Hot Chocolate Ice Cream combines the richness of traditional hot chocolate with the warmth of holiday spices, creating a cool, creamy version of a winter favorite. Cinnamon, nutmeg, and a hint of cayenne add warmth to the chocolatey base, making this ice cream a comforting yet refreshing holiday treat.

Ingredients:

- 1 1/2 cups whole milk
- 1 1/2 cups heavy cream
- 3/4 cup granulated sugar
- 1/4 cup unsweetened cocoa powder
- 4 oz dark chocolate, finely chopped

- 1/2 tsp cinnamon
- 1/4 tsp ground nutmeg
- 1/8 tsp ground cloves
- 1/8 tsp cayenne pepper (adjust to taste)
- 1 tsp vanilla extract

Instructions:

1. **Heat the Milk and Cream**:

   o In a medium saucepan, combine the milk, heavy cream, and half of the sugar. Heat over medium heat, stirring occasionally, until the mixture begins to steam but does not boil.

2. **Mix in the Cocoa and Spices**:

   o Whisk in the cocoa powder, cinnamon, nutmeg, cloves, and cayenne pepper. Continue to whisk until the cocoa powder and spices are fully dissolved.

3. **Prepare the Chocolate Base**:

   o Place the chopped dark chocolate in a large heatproof bowl. Pour the hot milk mixture over the chocolate and let it sit for a couple of minutes. Then, whisk until the chocolate is melted and smooth.

4. **Add Vanilla and Adjust Spices**:

   o Stir in the vanilla extract, and taste to see if you'd like to adjust the spice level. The cayenne adds a subtle heat, which you can increase or decrease based on your preference.

5. **Chill the Mixture**:

- o Cover the chocolate mixture with plastic wrap, pressing it directly onto the surface to prevent a skin from forming. Refrigerate for at least 4 hours or until completely chilled.

6. **Churn and Freeze**:

- o Pour the chilled chocolate mixture into an ice cream maker and churn according to the manufacturer's instructions, about 20-25 minutes.

7. **Freeze for a Firmer Texture**:

- o Transfer the ice cream to an airtight container and freeze for an additional 2-3 hours for a firmer texture. Serve scoops topped with mini marshmallows or a sprinkle of cinnamon for a festive touch.

Spiced Hot Chocolate Ice Cream is a delightful frozen twist on hot chocolate that combines the flavors of cinnamon and cayenne with rich chocolate, giving you the warmth and depth of hot chocolate in a cold, creamy treat. It's a fun way to surprise guests and pairs wonderfully with cookies or cakes for a complete holiday dessert.

Cranberry Sorbet and Spiced Hot Chocolate Ice Cream are both festive, flavorful treats that add a refreshing twist to traditional holiday flavors. The tangy, citrusy cranberry sorbet balances rich holiday meals, while the spicy hot chocolate ice cream satisfies chocolate lovers with its smooth texture and warming spices. Both desserts are perfect for holiday gatherings, adding an elegant, unexpected touch to the season's celebrations.

Chapter 8: Holiday Pies and Tarts

Pies and tarts have long been a staple of holiday celebrations, bringing comfort and sweetness to family gatherings. Classic flavors like pumpkin, pecan, and apple get a holiday upgrade with inventive ingredients and textures that bring new depth to familiar tastes. This chapter explores three standout holiday pies and tarts, each with its unique spin on tradition.

Classic Pumpkin Pie with a Twist

Pumpkin pie is an autumn and winter classic, but adding a twist can elevate this dessert into something truly special for the Christmas season. By incorporating a layer of spiced caramel and a ginger snap crust, this pumpkin pie brings added warmth and complexity, making it both nostalgic and refreshingly unique.

90

Ingredients:

For the Crust:

- 1 1/2 cups ginger snap cookie crumbs (about 30 cookies)
- 1/4 cup granulated sugar
- 6 tbsp unsalted butter, melted

For the Caramel Layer:

- 1/2 cup brown sugar
- 1/4 cup heavy cream
- 2 tbsp unsalted butter
- 1/2 tsp ground cinnamon
- 1/4 tsp ground nutmeg

For the Pumpkin Filling:

- 1 15-oz can pumpkin puree
- 3/4 cup heavy cream
- 1/2 cup granulated sugar
- 1/4 cup brown sugar
- 2 large eggs
- 1 tsp vanilla extract
- 1 tsp ground cinnamon
- 1/2 tsp ground ginger
- 1/4 tsp ground nutmeg
- 1/4 tsp ground cloves
- 1/4 tsp salt

Instructions:

1. **Prepare the Crust:**

- o Preheat your oven to 350°F (175°C). In a medium bowl, combine the ginger snap crumbs and sugar. Add the melted butter and stir until the crumbs are moistened.

- o Press the mixture firmly into the bottom and up the sides of a 9-inch pie pan. Bake the crust for 8-10 minutes, then let it cool while you prepare the filling.

2. **Make the Caramel Layer**:

- o In a small saucepan, combine the brown sugar, heavy cream, and butter. Heat over medium-low heat, stirring constantly, until the mixture is smooth and begins to thicken, about 5 minutes. Remove from heat and stir in the cinnamon and nutmeg.

- o Pour the caramel over the cooled crust and spread it evenly. Let it cool slightly.

3. **Prepare the Pumpkin Filling**:

- o In a large bowl, whisk together the pumpkin puree, heavy cream, granulated sugar, brown sugar, eggs, vanilla, cinnamon, ginger, nutmeg, cloves, and salt until smooth.

4. **Assemble and Bake**:

- o Pour the pumpkin filling over the caramel layer in the crust, spreading it evenly.

- o Bake the pie for 50-60 minutes, or until the filling is set but slightly jiggly in the center. Cool the pie on a wire rack.

5. **Serve**:

   ○ Serve the pie with a dollop of whipped cream and a sprinkle of cinnamon, if desired. The ginger snap crust and caramel layer add a rich twist, balancing beautifully with the spiced pumpkin filling.

This unique take on pumpkin pie blends the flavors of ginger and caramel for a comforting, decadent holiday dessert that's sure to impress.

Chocolate Pecan Pie

Chocolate Pecan Pie is a holiday favorite with a deliciously indulgent twist. By adding chocolate, this pie gains a luscious, rich flavor that perfectly complements the nutty pecans. The result is a dessert that combines the best of classic pecan pie and chocolate flavors, offering a rich, gooey filling and a satisfying crunch.

Ingredients:

For the Crust:

- 1 9-inch unbaked pie crust (store-bought or homemade)

For the Filling:

- 1 cup dark corn syrup
- 3/4 cup granulated sugar
- 1/2 cup unsalted butter, melted
- 3 large eggs
- 1 tbsp vanilla extract
- 1/4 tsp salt
- 1 cup semi-sweet chocolate chips

- 1 1/2 cups pecan halves

Instructions:

1. **Prepare the Crust:**

   o Preheat your oven to 350°F (175°C). If using a homemade crust, roll it out and fit it into a 9-inch pie dish, trimming and crimping the edges as desired.

2. **Prepare the Filling:**

   o In a large bowl, whisk together the corn syrup, sugar, melted butter, eggs, vanilla extract, and salt until smooth and well combined.

3. **Add Chocolate and Pecans:**

   o Sprinkle the chocolate chips evenly across the bottom of the pie crust, followed by a layer of pecan halves. Pour the filling over the chocolate and pecans, spreading it evenly.

4. **Bake:**

   o Bake the pie for 55-60 minutes, or until the filling is set and slightly puffed in the center. If the crust begins to brown too quickly, cover the edges with foil.

5. **Cool and Serve:**

   o Let the pie cool completely on a wire rack before slicing. Serve with whipped cream or a scoop of vanilla ice cream.

This Chocolate Pecan Pie is decadent, rich, and perfect for chocolate lovers, offering a warm and satisfying dessert that brings together chocolate, pecans, and a touch of holiday sweetness.

8.3. Cranberry Apple Crumble Pie

Cranberry Apple Crumble Pie is a festive, fruity dessert that combines the sweet-tart flavors of apples and cranberries with a buttery crumble topping. This pie is a seasonal twist on traditional apple pie, incorporating cranberries for a pop of color and flavor. It's a cozy and visually appealing dessert that brings a touch of Christmas charm.

Ingredients:

For the Crust:

- 1 9-inch unbaked pie crust (store-bought or homemade)

For the Filling:

- 4 large apples (such as Granny Smith or Honeycrisp), peeled and thinly sliced
- 1 cup fresh or frozen cranberries
- 1/2 cup granulated sugar
- 1/4 cup brown sugar
- 2 tbsp all-purpose flour
- 1 tbsp lemon juice
- 1/2 tsp cinnamon
- 1/4 tsp nutmeg

For the Crumble Topping:

- 1/2 cup all-purpose flour
- 1/2 cup rolled oats
- 1/3 cup brown sugar
- 1/4 tsp cinnamon
- 1/4 cup unsalted butter, chilled and cubed

Instructions:

1. **Prepare the Crust**:

   o Preheat the oven to 375°F (190°C). Roll out the pie crust, fit it into a 9-inch pie dish, and set aside.

2. **Make the Filling**:

   o In a large bowl, combine the sliced apples, cranberries, granulated sugar, brown sugar, flour, lemon juice, cinnamon, and nutmeg. Toss to coat the apples and cranberries evenly.

3. **Prepare the Crumble Topping**:

   o In a medium bowl, combine the flour, oats, brown sugar, and cinnamon. Add the chilled butter and cut it into the mixture using a pastry cutter or your fingers until the mixture resembles coarse crumbs.

4. **Assemble the Pie**:

o Pour the apple-cranberry filling into the prepared pie crust, spreading it out evenly. Sprinkle the crumble topping evenly over the filling.

5. **Bake**:

o Bake the pie for 45-55 minutes, or until the filling is bubbly and the topping is golden brown. If the edges of the crust begin to brown too quickly, cover them with foil.

6. **Cool and Serve**:

o Let the pie cool slightly before serving. For extra indulgence, serve it warm with a scoop of vanilla ice cream or a dollop of whipped cream.

Cranberry Apple Crumble Pie is a delightful blend of flavors and textures, combining the sweetness of apples with the tartness of cranberries and the crunch of a buttery oat crumble. It's a show-stopping dessert that's sure to bring festive cheer to any gathering.

Mince Pie (Traditional British Christmas Pie)

Mince pies have been a British holiday favorite for centuries, offering a warm, spiced filling packed with dried fruits, spices, and often a splash of brandy. Traditionally enjoyed during the Christmas season, these pies bring a rich, nostalgic flavor, evoking the warmth and coziness of holiday gatherings. These small pies are perfect for serving individually, making them ideal for holiday parties or as a treat by the fire.

Ingredients:

For the Mince Filling:

- 1 cup raisins
- 1 cup currants
- 1/2 cup dried cranberries or cherries, chopped
- 1/2 cup dried apricots, chopped
- 1/2 cup brown sugar
- 1/2 tsp ground cinnamon
- 1/2 tsp ground nutmeg
- 1/4 tsp ground cloves
- 1/4 tsp allspice
- Zest of 1 orange
- Juice of 1 orange
- 1/4 cup brandy or rum (optional, but traditional)
- 1/2 cup unsalted butter, melted

For the Pastry:

- 2 cups all-purpose flour
- 1/4 cup granulated sugar
- 1/2 tsp salt
- 1 cup cold unsalted butter, cubed
- 1 large egg, beaten
- 1-2 tbsp ice-cold water (as needed)

Instructions:

1. **Prepare the Mince Filling:**

98

- o In a large bowl, combine the raisins, currants, dried cranberries or cherries, apricots, brown sugar, cinnamon, nutmeg, cloves, allspice, orange zest, orange juice, and brandy. Mix well, ensuring that the fruit is evenly coated with the spices.

- o Stir in the melted butter and let the mixture sit, covered, at room temperature for at least 1 hour. For the best flavor, allow it to rest overnight or up to 2 days in the fridge, letting the flavors meld.

2. **Prepare the Pastry**:

- o In a large mixing bowl, whisk together the flour, sugar, and salt. Add the cold butter and cut it into the flour mixture using a pastry cutter or your fingers until it resembles coarse crumbs.

- o Add the beaten egg and 1 tablespoon of ice-cold water, mixing gently. Add more water if needed until the dough begins to come together. Form the dough into a disk, wrap it in plastic wrap, and refrigerate for at least 30 minutes.

3. **Assemble the Mince Pies**:

- o Preheat the oven to 375°F (190°C) and grease a 12-cup muffin tin.

- o Roll out the chilled dough on a lightly floured surface to about 1/8-inch thickness. Cut out circles to line each muffin cup, pressing gently to fit the dough into each cup.

- o Fill each pastry cup with about 1 tablespoon of the mince filling. Then, cut smaller circles or festive shapes (like stars) to place over the top of each pie.

4. **Bake the Mince Pies**:

- o Bake for 20-25 minutes, or until the pastry is golden and the filling is bubbly. Let the pies cool in the tin for a few minutes before transferring them to a wire rack to cool completely.

5. **Serve**:

- o Serve warm or at room temperature, dusted with powdered sugar for a snowy, festive look. These pies are delightful on their own or paired with a dollop of whipped cream or brandy butter.

With their spiced, fruity filling and buttery crust, mince pies are an essential part of British holiday celebrations. The deep, aromatic flavors of the fruit filling make these small pies perfect for savoring by a warm fire.

8.5. Pear and Almond Tart

The Pear and Almond Tart, also known as Tarte Bourdaloue in France, is a sophisticated, elegant dessert featuring a buttery almond filling topped with tender poached pears. It's a lovely way to celebrate the season's harvest and adds a refined touch to holiday gatherings. This tart combines the delicate flavors of almond and pear, creating a dessert that's subtly sweet, creamy, and beautifully aromatic.

Ingredients:

For the Pastry Crust:

- 1 1/4 cups all-purpose flour
- 1/4 cup powdered sugar
- 1/4 tsp salt
- 1/2 cup unsalted butter, cold and cubed
- 1 large egg yolk
- 1-2 tbsp cold water (as needed)

For the Almond Filling (Frangipane):

- 1/2 cup unsalted butter, softened
- 1/2 cup granulated sugar
- 1 cup almond flour
- 2 large eggs
- 1 tsp vanilla extract
- 1/2 tsp almond extract
- 1 tbsp all-purpose flour

For the Poached Pears:

- 3 ripe but firm pears, peeled, halved, and cored
- 3 cups water
- 1/2 cup sugar
- 1 cinnamon stick
- 1 tsp vanilla extract
- Juice of 1 lemon

Instructions:

1. **Prepare the Pastry Crust**:

- o In a food processor, pulse together the flour, powdered sugar, and salt. Add the cubed butter and pulse until the mixture resembles coarse crumbs.

- o Add the egg yolk and pulse again. Gradually add cold water, one tablespoon at a time, until the dough starts to come together. Form the dough into a disk, wrap it in plastic, and refrigerate for at least 30 minutes.

2. **Poach the Pears**:

- o In a medium saucepan, combine the water, sugar, cinnamon stick, vanilla extract, and lemon juice. Bring to a simmer.

- o Add the pear halves and poach them for about 10-15 minutes, or until they're just tender. Remove the pears with a slotted spoon and let them cool. Slice each pear half lengthwise into thin slices, keeping the shape intact.

3. **Prepare the Almond Filling (Frangipane)**:

- o In a mixing bowl, cream the softened butter and sugar until light and fluffy. Add the eggs, one at a time, beating well after each addition.

- o Stir in the almond flour, vanilla extract, almond extract, and all-purpose flour until smooth and well combined.

4. **Assemble the Tart**:

- o Preheat the oven to 350°F (175°C). Roll out the chilled pastry dough and fit it into a 9-inch tart pan. Trim the edges and prick the base with a fork.

- o Spread the almond filling evenly over the tart crust. Arrange the pear halves decoratively on top of the almond filling, fanning each one slightly.

5. **Bake**:

- o Bake the tart for 40-45 minutes, or until the almond filling is set and golden around the edges. Allow the tart to cool in the pan.

6. **Serve**:

- o Serve the tart warm or at room temperature, dusted with powdered sugar or brushed with a bit of warmed apricot jam for a glossy finish. It pairs beautifully with a dollop of whipped cream or vanilla ice cream.

The Pear and Almond Tart is a stunning centerpiece that will impress holiday guests with its delicate flavors and elegant presentation. The almond frangipane is rich and creamy, while the poached pears add a refreshing sweetness that elevates this tart to something truly memorable.

Mince Pie and Pear and Almond Tart offer different but complementary flavors to a holiday table. The traditional British mince pies bring warmth, spice, and fruitiness, while the French-inspired Pear and Almond Tart introduces subtle sweetness and elegance. Both desserts are delightful options that highlight festive ingredients and are sure to become seasonal favorites in any holiday repertoire.

Chapter 9: Festive Breads and Savory Pastries

Breads and savory pastries are essential parts of holiday feasting. They provide versatility, adding both warmth and substance to holiday brunches, dinners, and gatherings. This chapter explores three delicious, easy-to-share recipes that bring festive flavors and textures to the holiday table. Perfect as appetizers, sides, or even edible gifts, these recipes will help make the season's meals feel even more complete.

Cheddar and Chive Biscuits

Cheddar and Chive Biscuits are savory, flaky, and packed with sharp cheddar flavor and a hint of fresh chives. These biscuits are easy to make and pair wonderfully with a holiday brunch, a hearty bowl of soup, or a festive dinner. Their light, buttery layers make them a crowd-pleaser and an excellent addition to any holiday bread basket.

Ingredients:

- 2 cups all-purpose flour
- 1 tbsp baking powder
- 1/2 tsp baking soda
- 1/2 tsp salt
- 1/4 cup cold unsalted butter, cubed
- 1 cup sharp cheddar cheese, grated
- 1/4 cup fresh chives, chopped
- 3/4 cup buttermilk (plus extra if needed)

Instructions:

1. **Preheat the Oven**:
   - Preheat your oven to 425°F (220°C). Line a baking sheet with parchment paper.

2. **Prepare the Dough**:

o   In a large mixing bowl, whisk together the flour, baking powder, baking soda, and salt. Add the cold butter cubes, using a pastry cutter or your fingers to cut the butter into the flour until the mixture resembles coarse crumbs.

3. **Add the Cheese and Chives**:

o   Stir in the grated cheddar cheese and chopped chives, mixing to distribute evenly.

4. **Add the Buttermilk**:

o   Make a well in the center of the flour mixture and pour in the buttermilk. Stir until just combined, being careful not to overwork the dough. If the dough is too dry, add a bit more buttermilk, one tablespoon at a time.

5. **Shape and Cut the Biscuits**:

o   Turn the dough out onto a floured surface and gently pat it into a 1-inch-thick rectangle. Using a biscuit cutter or a round cookie cutter, cut out rounds and place them on the prepared baking sheet.

6. **Bake**:

o   Bake the biscuits for 12-15 minutes, or until they are golden brown on top. Let them cool slightly on a wire rack.

7. **Serve**:

o   Serve the biscuits warm, with a spread of butter or even a dollop of cranberry chutney for an added holiday touch. These biscuits are also delicious paired with savory dishes or as part of a festive brunch.

The combination of sharp cheddar and fresh chives adds a depth of flavor, while the flaky layers make these biscuits irresistible. They're an easy-to-make, elegant addition to any holiday spread.

Sausage Rolls with a Holiday Twist

Sausage rolls are a beloved holiday favorite, and they're even better with a festive twist. In this version, we add holiday spices, dried cranberries, and a touch of caramelized onion to the sausage filling. Encased in flaky puff pastry, these rolls are perfect as an appetizer, brunch addition, or party snack.

Ingredients:

- 1 tbsp olive oil

- 1/2 cup onions, finely chopped

- 1 lb ground pork sausage

- 1/4 cup dried cranberries, finely chopped

- 1 tsp fresh thyme, chopped

- 1/2 tsp ground sage

- 1/4 tsp ground nutmeg

- 1/4 tsp ground black pepper

- 1/4 tsp salt

- 1 large egg, beaten (for egg wash)

- 1 package puff pastry, thawed

Instructions:

1. **Prepare the Filling:**
    - In a skillet, heat olive oil over medium heat. Add the onions and cook until they are softened and caramelized, about 8-10 minutes.
    - In a large bowl, combine the ground sausage, chopped dried cranberries, thyme, sage, nutmeg, pepper, and salt. Add the caramelized onions and mix well to combine.

2. **Prepare the Puff Pastry:**
    - Preheat your oven to 400°F (200°C). Line a baking sheet with parchment paper.
    - Roll out the puff pastry sheets on a lightly floured surface. Cut each sheet into rectangles, about 4 inches by 5 inches.

3. **Assemble the Sausage Rolls:**
    - Place a heaping tablespoon of the sausage mixture onto one end of each puff pastry rectangle. Roll the pastry over the filling, pinching the edges to seal.

> ○ Place the rolls on the prepared baking sheet, seam side down. Brush the tops with beaten egg to create a golden, shiny finish.

4. **Bake**:

> ○ Bake the sausage rolls for 20-25 minutes, or until the pastry is golden brown and the sausage is fully cooked.

5. **Serve**:

> ○ Serve warm as a delightful savory treat. These rolls are delicious on their own but can also be served with a side of cranberry sauce or Dijon mustard for dipping.

Adding cranberries, thyme, and holiday spices to traditional sausage rolls gives them a festive twist that's both unique and flavorful. The contrast of sweet and savory flavors makes these sausage rolls perfect for holiday gatherings and a standout addition to any appetizer spread.

Herb and Garlic Focaccia

Herb and Garlic Focaccia is a flavorful Italian-inspired bread with a soft, chewy texture and a fragrant, crispy crust. Topped with fresh herbs, garlic, and a drizzle of olive oil, this focaccia is perfect for serving alongside soups, salads, or holiday spreads. It's an easy-to-make bread that will impress guests and complement any savory holiday dish.

Ingredients:

- 2 1/4 tsp active dry yeast

- 1 1/4 cups warm water (110°F/43°C)
- 2 tbsp olive oil, plus more for drizzling
- 3 1/4 cups all-purpose flour
- 1 1/2 tsp salt
- 3 cloves garlic, finely minced
- Fresh rosemary, thyme, and oregano, chopped (about 1-2 tbsp of each)
- Sea salt flakes, for sprinkling

Instructions:

1. **Activate the Yeast:**

   o In a large bowl, combine the warm water, yeast, and 1 tablespoon of olive oil. Stir and let sit for 5-10 minutes, or until the yeast becomes foamy.

2. **Make the Dough:**

   o Add the flour and salt to the yeast mixture and mix until a rough dough forms. Transfer the dough to a lightly floured surface and knead for about 8-10 minutes, until the dough is smooth and elastic.

3. **Let the Dough Rise:**

   o Place the dough in a lightly oiled bowl, cover it with a damp cloth, and let it rise in a warm place for 1-1.5 hours, or until doubled in size.

4. **Shape and Add Toppings:**

   o Preheat the oven to 400°F (200°C). Punch down the dough and press it into a large, oiled baking sheet or cast-iron skillet.

THE MAGIC OF HOLIDAY BAKING

- o Use your fingers to dimple the surface of the dough. Drizzle with olive oil, then sprinkle the minced garlic and chopped herbs evenly over the top. Sprinkle a few pinches of sea salt flakes for extra flavor.

5. **Bake**:

- o Bake the focaccia for 20-25 minutes, or until it is golden brown and crispy on the edges. Let it cool slightly on a wire rack.

6. **Serve**:

- o Serve warm or at room temperature. This focaccia pairs beautifully with a charcuterie board, olive oil for dipping, or as a side to a holiday meal.

Herb and Garlic Focaccia brings aromatic flavors and a perfect crunch to any holiday gathering. With its soft, airy interior and herb-topped crust, this bread is both rustic and refined, ideal for holiday feasts and easy to make ahead of time.

Savory Puff Pastry Twists

Savory Puff Pastry Twists are a delightful snack that combines flaky puff pastry with a variety of savory fillings. These twists can be easily customized with your favorite flavors, from Parmesan and herbs to pesto or sun-dried tomato. They're perfect for dipping into soups, adding to cheese boards, or serving as a festive appetizer at holiday gatherings. Not only are they visually appealing, but they're also easy to make and serve, making them a quick and impressive choice.

Ingredients:

- 1 sheet puff pastry, thawed
- 1/2 cup Parmesan cheese, grated
- 1 tbsp fresh rosemary, chopped
- 1 tbsp fresh thyme leaves
- 1 tsp garlic powder
- 1/2 tsp sea salt
- 1 large egg, beaten (for egg wash)
- Freshly ground black pepper (optional)
- Optional filling variations: pesto, sun-dried tomato paste, or olive tapenade

Instructions:

1. **Prepare the Puff Pastry:**

   o Preheat your oven to 400°F (200°C). Line a baking sheet with parchment paper.

   o Roll out the puff pastry on a lightly floured surface to smooth any creases. If you're using a second layer of puff pastry for filled twists, roll it out to match the size of the first sheet.

2. **Add the Toppings:**

   o Lightly brush the puff pastry with beaten egg to help the toppings adhere. Sprinkle the Parmesan cheese, chopped rosemary, thyme, garlic powder, and sea salt evenly over the surface.

   o For added flavor, sprinkle black pepper to taste. If using a filling (such as pesto or olive tapenade), spread a thin layer on half of the pastry and then fold the other half on top.

3. **Cut and Twist**:

   ○ Using a pizza cutter or sharp knife, cut the puff pastry into strips about 1/2 to 3/4 inch wide.

   ○ Carefully twist each strip several times and place on the prepared baking sheet, pressing the ends slightly so they hold their shape. Brush the twists lightly with more beaten egg.

4. **Bake**:

   ○ Bake for 12-15 minutes, or until the twists are golden brown and puffed up. Keep an eye on them to avoid over-browning.

5. **Serve**:

   ○ Let the twists cool slightly on a wire rack. Serve warm or at room temperature with dips, cheese boards, or as a standalone savory snack.

Savory Puff Pastry Twists are a wonderfully adaptable appetizer that can be flavored to suit any palate. Their flaky texture and herbaceous notes make them a perfect addition to holiday gatherings, whether as an appetizer or an accompaniment to a charcuterie board.

Olive and Rosemary Bread

Olive and Rosemary Bread is a rustic, aromatic loaf inspired by Mediterranean flavors. It's a wonderful bread to serve as an appetizer with olive oil for dipping, as a side to holiday dinners, or as part of a festive bread basket. The combination of briny olives and fragrant rosemary creates a complex, satisfying taste, and the homemade nature of this bread adds a warm, personal touch to holiday meals.

Ingredients:

- 2 1/4 tsp active dry yeast
- 1 1/2 cups warm water (about 110°F/43°C)
- 1 tbsp honey or sugar
- 3 1/2 cups all-purpose flour (or bread flour), plus more for dusting
- 1/2 cup pitted Kalamata or black olives, roughly chopped
- 2 tbsp fresh rosemary, chopped
- 2 tbsp olive oil, plus more for brushing
- 1 1/2 tsp salt
- Sea salt flakes, for sprinkling

Instructions:

1. **Activate the Yeast**:

    o In a large mixing bowl, combine the warm water, yeast, and honey or sugar. Stir and let sit for 5-10 minutes, until the mixture becomes foamy. This indicates that the yeast is active.

2. **Mix the Dough**:

- Add the flour and salt to the yeast mixture and mix until a rough dough forms. Transfer the dough to a floured surface and knead for about 8-10 minutes, or until the dough is smooth and elastic.

- Gently knead in the chopped olives and rosemary until evenly distributed throughout the dough. Drizzle with olive oil and knead to incorporate it fully.

3. **Let the Dough Rise**:

- Place the dough in a lightly oiled bowl, cover it with a damp cloth, and let it rise in a warm place for 1-1.5 hours, or until doubled in size.

4. **Shape the Bread**:

- Once risen, punch down the dough and transfer it back to a floured surface. Shape it into a round or oval loaf, or divide it into two smaller loaves if desired.

- Place the loaf on a baking sheet lined with parchment paper. Cover with a cloth and let rise for another 30 minutes.

5. **Preheat the Oven**:

- Preheat your oven to 400°F (200°C). Just before baking, brush the top of the loaf with olive oil and sprinkle with sea salt flakes for added flavor and crunch.

6. **Bake**:

- ○ Bake the bread for 30-35 minutes, or until it is golden brown and sounds hollow when tapped on the bottom. Let the bread cool on a wire rack before slicing.

7. **Serve**:

- ○ Serve this bread warm with a drizzle of extra virgin olive oil or alongside a holiday cheese board. Its robust flavor pairs beautifully with soups, pasta dishes, or roasted meats.

The Olive and Rosemary Bread is a rustic, flavorful loaf that's perfect for holiday meals. The olives add bursts of saltiness, while the rosemary offers an earthy, festive aroma that enhances any holiday spread. This bread can also be sliced and toasted as an appetizer or served with festive dips.

Savory Puff Pastry Twists and Olive and Rosemary Bread add a special touch to holiday gatherings. The Puff Pastry Twists provide an easy-to-make, flaky, and customizable appetizer, while the Olive and Rosemary Bread offers a rustic, aromatic addition to a holiday feast. These breads and pastries bring balance to sweet treats and add substance to your holiday menu. Whether served as part of a bread basket, alongside main dishes, or on an appetizer board, they will make your holiday gatherings feel even more special and memorable.

Chapter 10: Creative Gift-Giving Ideas with Homemade Treats for the Christmas Season

Homemade treats can be a thoughtful and memorable way to show appreciation for friends, family, neighbors, and colleagues during the holiday season. The key to successful edible gifts lies in choosing recipes that are both delicious and suited for gifting, along with packaging that feels special and festive. This chapter guides you through everything you need to create beautiful, customized gifts with your homemade treats.

Choosing the Right Recipe for Gifting

When it comes to giving homemade treats, choosing the right recipe is essential. Look for recipes that are not only delicious but also easy to transport, store, and share. Certain types of baked goods hold up better than others, making them ideal for gifting.

Tips for Choosing Gifting Recipes:

- **Shelf-Stable Treats**: Recipes like cookies, biscotti, fudge, and candies tend to keep well without refrigeration, making them easy to pack and ship. These treats stay fresh for a longer period and can be enjoyed over several days.

- **Sturdy Items**: Fragile treats like meringues or delicate pastries may not withstand travel well. Choose items that are durable, such as shortbread, brownies, or nut clusters.

- **Seasonal Flavors**: Embrace the flavors of the season with recipes that feature ingredients like cinnamon, ginger,

117

nutmeg, peppermint, and chocolate. These festive flavors will enhance the holiday spirit of your gifts.

- **Easy to Portion**: Treats that can be divided into individual servings, such as cookies, truffles, or mini loaves, are ideal for gifting. They're easy to package and can be enjoyed in small portions.

- **Variety for Gifting Sets**: If you're assembling a gift box or hamper, consider including a variety of items, such as cookies, fudge, and spiced nuts, to provide a diverse range of flavors and textures.

Packaging Ideas: Jars, Boxes, and Bows

Packaging plays a vital role in creating a memorable gift experience. The right packaging makes homemade treats feel festive, special, and beautiful. Here are some creative ideas for presenting your treats:

Creative Packaging Ideas:

- **Mason Jars**: Perfect for candies, granola, and layered dry mixes like cookie or brownie jars. Simply layer the ingredients in a clear mason jar, seal with a festive fabric topper, and add a recipe tag.

- **Cellophane Bags**: Clear bags are ideal for cookies, brownies, and brittle. Tie them with a festive ribbon and label, making them easy to gift to multiple recipients or as part of a larger gift basket.

- **Gift Boxes and Tins**: Decorative boxes or tins are ideal for cookie assortments, fudge, or small cakes. Add parchment paper for a polished, bakery-style look, and secure with festive ribbons.

- **Decorative Bows and Ribbons**: A simple ribbon can transform plain packaging into a festive gift. Choose seasonal colors like red, green, gold, or silver, and use different textures, such as velvet or satin, for an added touch of elegance.

- **Recyclable or Reusable Packaging**: Consider eco-friendly packaging options like compostable boxes, reusable metal tins, or cloth wraps. These options are sustainable and add an extra layer of thoughtfulness to your gift.

- **Custom Gift Bags**: Personalize plain brown or white gift bags with holiday stamps, stencils, or markers. These bags can fit various items, from breads to cookies, and add a handmade touch.

How to Make a Christmas Cookie Box

A Christmas cookie box is a delightful gift that brings together a variety of holiday flavors and textures. Creating a cookie box is about choosing a diverse selection of cookies, arranging them beautifully, and adding festive touches for a presentation that's both charming and practical.

Steps to Create a Christmas Cookie Box:

1. **Select a Variety of Cookies**: Aim for at least three to five types of cookies, including different flavors, shapes, and textures. Consider including classic holiday cookies like

gingerbread, sugar cookies, chocolate crinkle cookies, and shortbread.

2. **Choose a Sturdy Box**: Select a box that's large enough to fit all your cookies without crowding. Divided gift boxes work well, or you can use small cupcake liners to separate the cookies and prevent them from shifting.

3. **Arrange the Cookies**: Arrange cookies by type, grouping similar colors and shapes together for an appealing look. Place larger, sturdier cookies on the bottom and layer lighter, delicate cookies on top.

4. **Add Festive Touches**: Line the box with parchment paper, tissue paper, or decorative holiday napkins. You can also add sprigs of rosemary or mini candy canes for a festive flair.

5. **Include a Personalized Note**: Write a short holiday greeting or a list of the cookies in the box. This adds a personal touch and lets the recipient know what they're enjoying.

6. **Seal and Decorate**: Close the box, securing it with a ribbon or bow. If using a transparent lid, you can place a holiday sticker or a festive tag on the outside.

A well-assembled Christmas cookie box is a beautiful gift that combines variety, flavor, and festive presentation. The different textures and colors make it a delightful holiday treat, perfect for family, friends, or neighbors.

Preparing Festive Gift Hampers

Gift hampers are versatile and allow you to combine a variety of homemade treats and small gifts in a single, personalized package. Preparing a festive gift hamper can be a thoughtful way to share holiday joy, with each item chosen to suit the recipient's tastes.

Steps to Prepare a Holiday Gift Hamper:

1. **Choose a Theme**: Decide on a theme, such as "Holiday Breakfast," "Sweet Treats," or "Baking Essentials." This will help guide your selection of items and create a cohesive gift.

2. **Select a Basket or Box**: Choose a large, sturdy basket or box as your base. For an eco-friendly option, consider using a wooden crate, a reusable shopping basket, or a decorative storage box that the recipient can keep.

3. **Add a Variety of Treats**: Include an assortment of homemade items, such as jam, spiced nuts, cookies, and flavored syrup, as well as small non-perishable items like teas, coffee, or a small jar of honey. Be sure to vary the flavors and types of items to keep the hamper exciting.

4. **Layer with Filler Material**: Use shredded paper, crinkled tissue, or cloth napkins to cushion the items. This filler adds volume to the hamper and helps prevent items from shifting.

5. **Arrange and Decorate**: Place taller items at the back and smaller items in the front for an organized, aesthetically pleasing look. Add holiday-themed accents, such as pine cones, ornaments, or sprigs of evergreen, to give the hamper a festive feel.

6. **Include a Note or Recipe Card**: A handwritten note or a card with your favorite holiday recipe is a lovely personal touch. It

can add an extra layer of sentiment, showing thoughtfulness and care.

Festive gift hampers are wonderful because they allow you to customize each gift to suit the recipient's preferences, while also adding a creative, holiday-themed presentation.

Personalized Labels and Tags

Adding personalized labels and tags to your homemade treats gives each gift a unique, memorable touch. Labels and tags not only enhance the visual appeal but also offer practical information, such as ingredients, serving suggestions, or special holiday messages.

Creative Ideas for Labels and Tags:

- **Handwritten Tags**: Simple, handwritten tags can give your gifts a rustic, homemade charm. Use craft paper, cut into holiday shapes like stars or trees, and write a short note or holiday greeting with a metallic pen.

- **Printable Labels**: There are many online resources where you can download or design festive labels. Look for designs with holiday colors and patterns that match your packaging theme.

- **Chalkboard Stickers**: Chalkboard stickers are an easy and stylish way to label jars or boxes. Use a chalk pen to write the treat's name or a short message.

- **Recipe Tags**: For treats like cookie mixes or cake-in-a-jar, include a small tag with the recipe or baking instructions. This allows the recipient to make the treat themselves and enjoy the holiday baking experience.

- **Holiday Stamps and Embossing**: If you're crafty, consider using holiday stamps, embossing powder, or even a gold foil pen to create elegant labels and tags. A personalized label will make each gift feel thoughtfully prepared and uniquely festive.

- **Ingredient and Allergy Information**: If you're gifting treats to people with dietary restrictions, it's a good idea to include ingredient lists or allergy warnings on the labels. This adds a thoughtful, considerate touch.

Creating personalized gifts with homemade treats can be a fulfilling and creative way to celebrate the holiday season. From choosing the perfect recipes to assembling, packaging, and labeling, each step allows you to add your own personal touch. These gifts are not only delicious but also heartfelt expressions of holiday joy and warmth. With a little preparation and creativity, your homemade treats will bring smiles to everyone on your gift list, making their holiday season all the more special.

Chapter 11: Conclusion and Final Baking Tips

As we reach the end of our Christmas holiday baking journey, it's time to reflect on the joy that holiday baking brings—both to those creating these delicious treats and to those lucky enough to enjoy them. Christmas baking isn't just about following recipes; it's about creating lasting memories, traditions, and flavors that evoke warmth, togetherness, and joy. In this conclusion, we'll cover some final baking tips to help you bring out the best in every recipe and to make your holiday baking experience as smooth and enjoyable as possible.

1. Embrace the Spirit of Holiday Baking

The Christmas season is a time for giving, sharing, and spending time with loved ones. When you bake during this time, approach it with a sense of fun and a willingness to be flexible. Mistakes happen, and sometimes things don't turn out exactly as planned, but it's all part of the experience. The true value of holiday baking is found in the memories made along the way—like laughing with family members, decorating cookies with kids, or packing up baked goods to give as thoughtful, homemade gifts.

124

Remember, the real "magic ingredient" in all holiday baking is the love and effort you put into each recipe. Whether it's a cake, a batch of cookies, or a carefully decorated pie, baking brings people together and gives everyone something special to remember.

2. Plan and Prep for Stress-Free Baking

As the holidays are already a busy time, planning ahead makes a huge difference in reducing stress and keeping baking fun. Revisit your holiday baking schedule and make a list of the recipes you'd like to tackle. Check your pantry for key ingredients, and stock up on essentials like flour, sugar, butter, eggs, and holiday spices. Consider preparing doughs or batters in advance if recipes allow, and store them in the freezer for quick baking later on.

For multi-step recipes or complex baked goods, break down each recipe into manageable parts. Prep all ingredients in advance, gather your tools, and read through the instructions carefully. When you're well-prepared, baking can feel like a calm and enjoyable ritual rather than a rushed task.

3. Troubleshoot with Confidence

Even with the best preparation, baking can sometimes present challenges. Cookies may spread more than expected, cakes may not rise as high, or pie crusts might shrink. When issues arise, remember they're all part of the learning process, and even experienced bakers encounter these moments. Don't be afraid to improvise or adjust recipes slightly based on what you're observing. And remember, many "mistakes" can actually lead to new and delicious discoveries!

If a batch of cookies is too soft, try popping them back in the oven briefly or chilling the dough before baking. If a cake didn't rise as much as expected, a dusting of powdered sugar or a festive glaze can still make it beautiful. Sometimes, the best results come from a little flexibility and creativity.

4. Presentation and Packaging Tips for the Perfect Gift

Part of what makes holiday baking special is how beautifully it can be presented and gifted to others. When giving baked goods as gifts, consider how you'll package them to make them look as delightful as they taste. Here are a few presentation ideas:

- **Decorative Tins or Boxes**: Fill festive tins or gift boxes with an assortment of cookies, truffles, or candies. Add tissue paper or wax paper between layers to prevent sticking.

- **Mason Jars and Ribbon**: For items like biscotti or bars, stack them in mason jars and tie with a colorful ribbon. You could even add a small tag with a personal note or recipe.

- **Gift Bags with Personalized Labels**: Holiday gift bags work well for larger treats like loaves or individual pastries. Personalized labels with a holiday message add a special touch.

If you're sending treats through the mail, take extra care with packaging to ensure your goodies arrive safely. Wrap each item individually in parchment or wax paper, and use cushioned packaging material to prevent movement during shipping.

5. Experiment and Add Personal Touches

Once you're comfortable with a recipe, don't hesitate to add your personal twist. Swap out nuts, adjust spices, or use different types of chocolates or fruits. Adding your own flair to each recipe not only makes it uniquely yours but also allows you to create flavors that perfectly suit you and your family.

Experimenting also gives you a chance to try out new techniques or flavors. If you've never tried making a braided bread or decorating a cake with piping, now's a great time to learn and expand your baking skills. Even a simple garnish, like a sprig of fresh rosemary or a sprinkle of edible glitter, can make your baked goods feel festive and sophisticated.

6. Savor the Experience

The holiday season passes quickly, so take time to enjoy the process of baking, decorating, and sharing. Don't rush—play holiday music in the background, light some candles, and savor the aroma of spices and sweets filling your kitchen. If possible, involve family members or friends in the baking process; it's a wonderful way to bond and create shared memories. Remember that each treat you make is a little piece of holiday cheer that you're crafting with your own hands.

When it's time to serve your baked goods, present them with pride, knowing the effort and love you've poured into every item. These moments—like sharing a warm cookie or a slice of cake with loved ones—are what make holiday baking truly meaningful.

7. Keep Traditions Alive and Create New Ones

Every family has its own holiday traditions, and baking often plays a significant role. Cherish these traditions and pass them down to younger generations. If you grew up with a family fruitcake recipe or a particular gingerbread cookie recipe, consider inviting children or family members to help you make it, sharing the story behind each tradition.

At the same time, don't be afraid to start new traditions that reflect your tastes and style. Maybe it's creating a hot chocolate bar with homemade marshmallows or hosting a cookie decorating party each year. Traditions make the holiday season meaningful, and baking offers a perfect opportunity to create those lasting rituals.

Baking is a beautiful way to celebrate the season, combining creativity, patience, and love. With the right preparation, a touch of flexibility, and a spirit of joy, holiday baking can become a cherished part of your Christmas celebrations. Every treat you create has the potential to spark joy and bring warmth to someone's day. From cookies and cakes to breads and candies, these recipes are more than just food—they're an expression of love, kindness, and the magic of the season.

As you close this book and embark on your holiday baking adventures, remember that each recipe is just a starting point. The memories, connections, and joy you create along the way are the true rewards of baking. Here's to a wonderful, delicious, and joy-filled Christmas baking season!

Made in United States
Cleveland, OH
19 November 2024

10808688R00075